Art of Joyful Living

Pt. Gopal Sharma, B.E.

DIAMOND BOOKS
www.diamondbooks.in

Publisher : **Diamond Pocket Books (P) Ltd.**
X-30, Okhla Industrial Area,
Phase-II, New Delhi-110020
Phone : 011-40712200
E-mail : wecare@diamondbooks.in
Website : www.diamondbooks.in
Edition : 2025
Printed By : Repro (India)

Art of Joyful Living
Author - *Pt. Gopal Sharma,* B.E.

Art of Joyful Living

Lord Shri Krishna has helped me to truly enjoy life, at each and every moment, devoid of fear.

I may not know, what lies ahead of me, but what I do know is that, He has meticulously laid down every step of the path for me.

This is enough for me to know & continue to enjoy the life of abundance.

-Pt. Gopal Sharma, B.E.

About the Author

Pt. Gopal Sharma, an engineer turned Astro-Vaastu expert, was born in a revered family of Vedic Scholars & Spiritual Healers.

During his association of many decades, as a technical/Economic Adviser with a leading Bank, Pt. Gopal Sharma had been deeply involved in the establishment/ expansion and revival of numerous business/ industrial enterprises.

To spread our rich ancient heritage, even to enlightened people of other religion, Pandit ji has been selflessly engaged in:

- Publishing useful information on various subjects in different Magazines & Newspapers including Tahthaastu (USA), Mystique World (UK), Nirogdham, Future Samachar, Life-Positive, Khaleej Times, Gulf News, The Pioneer, Hindustan Times, Times of India, Indian Express, etc.
- Giving Consultancy on Astrology, Vaastu & Pyramid Power through Radio at Dubai, Australia, Canada & various TV channels including DOORDARSHAN, INDIA TV, JAIN TV, ZEE-TV, AASTHA CHANNEL, TV ASIA (USA), etc.

- Organizing/contributing to various workshops, seminars and giving consultancy in various parts of the world including Singapore, Dubai, UK, Malaysia, Canada, Saudi Arabia, Hongkong, USA, Swedan, South Africa, Australia, etc.

Pt. Gopal Sharma was also consulted by the Government of U.P. for planning the entire TRONICA CITY; the prestigious 1600 acre residential cum industrial complex; which proved a phenomenal success. His services were also utilized by the erstwhile Chief Minister of Orissa for conducting research about all the leading temples in the state.

At present, he is an eminent technical/management & financial consultant for many large industrial/business houses including Hellmann, Birlas, Piramals, United Shippers, Thapars, Jindals, Surya, Prakash Pipes, Action Group, House of Chemicals, Luthra & Luthra Law Offices, Pasco Automobiles, Sleepwell, Swiss Auto, Sahni Tyres, Gautam & Gautam Architects, Deepak Fertilizer & Chemicals, Baraza and Sassy-Spoon Chain of Restaurants, Choice Group, Piramal Group, Rohit Bal Group of Industries, Marriott Hotel USA, Ansal Group of Compnies, Neeco Jaiswal Group of Companies Raipur, AVG Logistics Ltd., Nainik Group of Companies Nagpur, Patanjali Yogpeeth & many leading Nationalized banks.

Besides Vice-President of All India Federation of Astrologer's societies, which has 73 centres across the Globe, he is the founder President of Institute of Vaastu & Joyful Living, engaged in doing research & experiments on the basic principles of various ancient sciences and propagating the exhaustive guidelines, exhibited in original texts; for the welfare of human beings.

Through the Corporate Office of the Institute at Delhi and various contacts abroad, Pt. Gopal Sharma is presently adding peace, prosperity & happiness in the lives of people by giving consultancy & conducting numerous courses on various holistic sciences by regular/part-time classes; as also by correspondence.

Under the realm of this institute, with the help of his team, Pandit ji has thousands of regular satisfied clients spread all over the globe; including those living in Malaysia, Singapore, Seychelles, Sri Lanka, Nepal, Japan, Lebanon, Nigeria, Canada, USA, Australia, Sweden, Kuwait, UAE, Oman, Mauritius, Greece, France, South Africa, Zambia, Botswana and UK.

He has also been felicitated with several medals and prestigious awards selflessly promoting this edifice science including the Millennium Vaastu Shastri Award by ISKON, Bhaskar Award by Bharat Nirman, Atma Jyoti Award by HUDCO & Sir Ganga Ram Hospital and Maharishi Shaunak Award at Jammu University, for successfully motivating thousands of people from all fields of life; across the globe.

He has to his credit 42 books including many bestsellers in Hindi, English, German, Greece & French on various holistic subjects. Based on his published material, he has also been awarded the DOCTORATE IN VAASTU SCIENCE by the Open University at Sri Lanka.

-Arun Bansal
President
All India Federation of Astrologers Society (Regd)

******

Discover your inner power and manifest the magical life you were born to live! The book offers practical, cheerful advice and simple guided exercises to support you in harnessing your energy, overcoming your limitations, and finding your happiest, most authentic self. Continuous practice of the simple guidelines, will equip you with the everyday magic skills and knowledge, you need in several areas:

- *Manifesting what you want, love, money & glitter.*

- *Choosing joy and living a life of magic & Gratitude.*

- *Recognizing the signs from the Universe you're receiving every day.*

- *Communicating with the Universe and accepting Divine assistance.*

- *Strategies for increasing your "daily magic" and your "life magic".*

- *Your life is meant to be one of wishes granted and dreams come true. Discover the manifesting magic within you to make that happen!*

******

Gratitude

Readily acceptance of numerous editions of the book **"Srishti Ka Khazana"** by people inspired me to compile, the feedback with its English Version. The project was made possible with the constant help, research work and great vision of Dr. S.R. Jaipuria Ji.

I am grateful to Sh. Georgy Bhaala, Chief Editor, Tathaastu (the leading Holistic Magazine of USA) who have been immensely helpful in organizing our numerous conferences/seminars/get-togethers in India, Sweden, South-Africa, Hong-Kong, London & different parts of US and Canada.

I am really indebted to his Divine Grace Sri Sri Ravishankarji and His Holiness Yogrishi Swami Ramdevji for their affection and support, showered on our various projects in various parts of the world.

I would also like to offer my honest appreciation to my better half Smt. Laxmi Sharma, without whose dedicated and selfless co-operation, the achievements of this life would not have been possible.

I also sincerely acknowledge the pains and interest taken by Shri Narender Kumar Verma Ji, Chairman Diamond Group of Publications, whose continuous motivation was vital in the presentation of this rare treatise.

At last, my deepest gratitude to the Universe for inspiring me with such a special project, and for guiding me through every step of its creation & presentation.

-Pt. Gopal Sharma, B.E.
Email: ptgopal@yahoo.com
website: www.ivjl.com

Contents

Chapter-1

Power of Thoughts

You can achieve anything & everything in your life, whatever you want, whether it is small or big. Believe me, you can definitely get what you desire.

- Aspire a luxurious apartment
- Want to be a millionaire
- Seeking success in life
- Looking for love and respect from all

If you know the technique, it is so simple.

Think it, Feel it, Receive it.

Seemingly impossible tasks are accomplished, Miracles happen every day! Money showers like rain over night, patients get cured in a moment, spoilt relations turn into a warm hug!

There is one and only one universal truth, whether it is Asia, Africa, Europe, USA, Australia or any other continent and it is one simple truth that you will achieve whatever you think, with a firm belief.

Do you know why some people are so rich? It is because they think only of richness.

It has also been noticed many a times, that a rich person becomes poor & over a period of time becomes rich again. Do you know why?

This is because previously they used to think only of richness. However, having become rich, they thought of losing all the money. As they started thinking so they became poor; becoming poor they were free from all worries and started thinking of richness. Their thoughts fulfilled their desire and they grew rich again. It may seem very difficult, but it is very simple & this thought process is one of the basic principles of Nature.

Many times you are worried or unhappy. You may be sad due to some reason, but the more you think about it, more you feel distressed. When we think of adversities, more and more thoughts of adversities and difficulties start accumulating around us. Within minutes, your soul gets filled with sorrows & sadness and your condition starts deteriorating in all spheres of life. Therefore, in order to progress in life, always keep positive views in your mind. Always think and concentrate on the target that you wish to achieve.

You will become what you aspire. So far whatever good or bad has occurred to you, it is all due to your way of thinking. Hence firmly believe in the right thinking process outcome & let the universe do the rest, for you.

If the channel is not of your liking, you just change it; similarly you can easily maintain only positive thoughts in your mind.

Adverse & undesirable thoughts, if allowed to keep running in the mind, can ruin your life. If a thought is not of your liking, change it immediately. Whatever you do not want in your life, do not allow it to enter your mind and even if it comes, remove it immediately; by replacing it with a positive thought of celebration & pure joy.

If you think in a negatively that you DO NOT want this or that, then it will definitely come to you. So don't think of anything which you don't need or you do not want.

If you think of prosperity and happiness, you will get showered with happiness and prosperity. If you think positive, only then positive will happen. It is the best practical way of avoiding undesired happenings in life.

What is the most natural drawback of a human being?

Most people concentrate on a thing that they don't want or don't need.

- I Don't want to live in poverty!
- I Don't want to face adversities!
- I Should not fall ill!
- Nobody offers me respect and honour!

Instead of this negative thinking, think assertively. Repeat and remind yourself that :

- I Want richness and I am rich already!
- I Want comforts and happiness I am happy!
- I Want good health and robust body, I am robust and healthy!
- I Want respect and am floating in peace!

Nature does not know whether what you wish is good or bad. It simply fulfills your desires. Nature cannot discriminate between positive and negative. If you think of loans or debts, Nature will help you to get drown in sorrow of debts; because you were only thinking of that.

Remember that Nature is obedient to you. It is always at your command and obeys you blindly. It offers you all that you aspire. If you repeat to yourself - "I should not get late, I should not get late." Nature will pick up the theme that your arc indeed aspiring to be late, your stress is on word late, so Nature will fully help you to be late.

Instead of this negative ideology or negative thought you should say, "I have to reach in time, I will reach in time." Visualize that you have already reached in time and really feel grateful to the Universe.

If you stress on something, either good or bad, it will definitely come to you. This law of Nature keeps on working round the clock, 24 hours; whether you agree or NOT. If you think over it and accept this law, you may become one of the most powerful person.

When you think of your past, either good or bad, at that moment, Nature also keeps listening to your past. When you think of future, even then, the Nature is listening to you. Always remember that the stream of thoughts keep flowing in your mind, while you are busy talking with anybody or enjoying TV or scanning newspaper or reading messages on your mobile - you are always continuously in the process of thinking. The only time when you are relieved of conscious thinking, is the time of deep sleep. Hence, for a brighter future, always bring good thoughts in your mind before you go to sleep. Keep calm and be thankful to the enormous virtues in your life.

Always remember that your pattern of thinking is your future; as your current thought process is creating your future. Let your faith be bigger than your fear.

There is an old proverb - **"As you sow, so shall you reap!"** In other words "as you think, so shall be your future" since your thoughts are the seeds of your future. Good thoughts will form good future and evil thoughts will lead you to an uncomfortable situation.

When you make complaints to yourself or to others, then Nature helps you to weave a vicious circle of complaints around you. If you listen to the sorrowful stories of others and rethink over it or show sympathy with them or even pay a positive nod, it means that you are attracting those miseries and sorrows to your life. The result will be that you will soon find a lots of reasons to start complaining about yourself or your life.

***Eckhart Tolle**, the celebrity author of "Practicing the Power of Now" also says "When you complain, you make yourself a victim. Leave the situation or change the situation or accept it. All else is madness."*

So the best advice is neither complain, nor listen to complaints.

There is a universal law that every action has an equal and opposite reaction. As you strike the tennis ball on the wall, it comes back to you with the same force. Similarly, our thoughts and assumptions are like a tennis ball; the more we concentrate on them, more powerfully they surround us.

Now, as you know the secret of happiness, you can adopt it in your life. **With the change of thoughts, you can change your life.** The man who thinks of success, will always achieve success.

Believe me, your life is in your own hands. It makes no difference what you have done up till now and what has happened in the past. You should start controlling your thoughts just now and it will bring changes in your life. You should never let negative thoughts enter your mind, never think that ***"all is over and no progress can ever come into my life."*** If you are keeping negative and pessimistic thoughts in mind, naturally you life will become gloomy & full of unhappiness. Please remember that a small happening or a small seed of positive thought can change your entire life.

Up till now you were not aware about the power of your own thoughts. Since you have realized the power you hold in yourself, you will feel that you have awakened from a deep and sound sleep, and have known the immense strength of your inner power.

Still even if you are not convinced, do not discard this theory. As you utilize electricity and enjoy optimum gain out of it; without knowing how it is created. Similarly you can enjoy optimum benefit from this unfailing law of Nature. Here and now take a pledge that only good and hopeful thoughts will enter your mind.

Please remember that a single good thought is many a times more powerful than thousand evil thoughts. Do not worry that you have accumulated unhappiness and sorrows in your mind. Be enthusiastic from today itself, like a burning candle in a dark room, your one single positive thought is good enough to destroy all sadness and pessimism.

- Keep your mind cool.
- Control your thoughts.
- Make it a habit to always spread smile and happiness.
- Meditate for at least 10 minutes daily in a comfortable and peaceful posture.

Repeating the above process daily, you will be able to discard evil thoughts and stop them from coming into your mind. You assert yourself, "I am the lord of my thoughts, only positive thoughts will get the place in my mind." Keep repeating these words, again and again; and gradually your negative thoughts and grief will vanish for ever.

You may be surprised to know that in a day almost 50-60 thousands thoughts crop up in the mind. Most of them irritate or frighten you, or cause distress leaving you tired. On the other hand when good and joyful thoughts pass through your mind, they rejuvenate your mind and body. If you feel joyous or in a state of happiness, it means positive and beautiful thoughts are sprouting in your mind. It is the universal truth that you can't have two states of mind i.e. you can either be happy or sad. You can't be both, So you better start cultivating happiness from now on. Every smile, every loving word, every kind action are reflections of the beauty of your heart and soul.

If you are in distress you will attract more stress towards yourself. If you are joyous, more and more joy will keep flowing towards you.

When you are happy you are always enriched with more enthusiasm, fervor, thankfulness, love and emotions of gratitude. Try to make a practice that these thoughts keep arising in your mind. When you feel joy, it indicates that you are nurturing brighter and safer future, which shall lead you to a right path. If you remain frightened and worried, it means you are inviting heaps of worry & further adversities.

From this moment onwards, start asserting and commanding yourself that:-

- I am healthy & happy.
- I am self sufficient and rich enough.
- I am surrounded by love, humbleness and tranquility.

Former President of India, Abdul Kalam Azad once rightly said, *"Heart is not a basket for keeping tension and sadness. It is a golden box for keeping roses of happiness and sweet memories."*

Your mind will always believe everything you tell it; hence, Feed it with faith. Feed it with truth. Feed it with love.

There is one truth that can help you. This truth is easy, simple & can be applied anywhere in the world. In case, you are trapped in sadness then immediately start singing your favorite song which has a positive sense; you can hum in you mind or best you can also listen to a joyful songs & peaceful music. This will allow you to relax & help you get in touch with your soul, thereby making you see life with clarity & a sense of purpose. As you do this, close your eyes and try to remember some joyful moments of your life.

As you feel relaxed, choose a peaceful place & with a very kind heart, pronounce the word 'AUM'. It is this word 'AUM' that has been confirmed by NASA as the most powerful word in the universe. The very pronunciation of this word not only burns bad Karma but can also change the destined path of life. It touches the deepest core of your consciousness & makes you see life with a whole new perspective. It makes you see your faults thereby giving you a chance to correct YOURSELF first & it is only then that you find yourself in a whole new world. A world that you never thought existed. A new place for your mind to reside in. A better place to be in. Because precisely, you only exist in your mind & if you are able to change then you can change anything in the world.

Sit & Relax. Take out some time and say 'AUM'.You can do so even while feeling troubled or anxious anywhere out. Just say 'AUM'& you will be fine.

Sometimes the best thing you can do is not to think, not to wonder, not to imagine, not to obsess, have faith that everything will work out for the best. There is a basic rule/law that - like attracts like. If you habitually think optimistically and positively, your thinking sets creative forces in motion - and success instead of eluding you, will naturally/effortlessly flow towards you.

We all know that love is the strongest feeling in universe. It is the most powerful emotion. When your thoughts are fully blended with love, then you can love the whole world and the entire world will love you as they love Swami Vivekanand or Mother Teresa.

You are beneficiary of this seed (thought) of love. The more you allow the feelings and thoughts of love to enter your mind, more energy and power will get generated in you. Train your mind to see good in every situation. You will realize whole Nature is helping you to fulfill your desires. Soon, you will start feeling that whatever you expect, is at your command.

"Blessings are everywhere. We just need positive thoughts to notice them."

Up till now you were feeling that life is full of miseries and bed of thorns, but you are responsible for your happiness. Infact, you create it, you attract it, you manifest it. You are the architect of your life because it is you who choose your thoughts, your perceptions and your reactions to your thoughts. You possess all the tools needed to expand your awareness, to orchestrate the evolution of your consciousness, to choose happiness, to choose love. You are powerful enough to create the life you deserve.

Believe, things will take care of themselves, if you just focus on your mission, on you goals, with a firm belief that you will certainly get whatever you sincerely put efforts for. You can't win in life if you are losing in your mind. Change your thoughts and it will change your life.

❐

Chapter-2

Miracles of Will Power, Faith & Love

You are Aladdin and Nature is the Gin of wishes in the lamp of Aladdin. As soon as you desire something the lamp ignites and the Gin of wishes and desires comes out of the lamp. When he comes out of the lamp he says, "I am at your command my Lord! I will do whatever you say, I will bring whatever you wish!" The result of your thought process does not differentiate between what is harmful or what is beneficial to you. The process simply assures whatever you need will be at your feet. Gin will not ask any question! He will simply obey you and provide you with what you want, because it is you who is the lord of Gin and Gin is capable of fulfilling all your desires.

Three things are to be done to get something -

1. Ask for it,
2. Believe that you will receive it,
3. Love it when you receive it.

Nature works in similar fashion to that of an e-commerce company. You select a watch you like. You order the watch & pay for it. There is an immediate ENERGY EXCHANGE. It is now confirmed that you will receive the watch. There is no denying, no doubt, no apprehension about it.

So when it comes to intangible desires or wishes nature works in similar fashion. You just have to believe that you will get it.

Infact, you have to start assuming that you already own that particular wish. From right now, believe that you have received your desired item.

Nature will certainly make a way where there seems to be no way at the moment. It works in a way we cannot see. Nature is able to do more than one can ever imagine. Keep your trust in Nature, and Nature will reward you for the trust you bestow upon it.

Nature can hear you in your chaos. It hears your whispers too. Nature is fond of speed, don't delay. Don't give a second thought. Never ever doubt the Power of Nature and you will get it faster than you can ever imagine.

As soon as you feel enthusiastic and inspired for any task, do it instantaneously. Any task committed with inspiration and dedication yields wonderful results. Develop a habit to do all the jobs with fervor and joy.

There is one condition, though. For achieving whatever you desire, you must have clarity in mind about what you need. If you ask something from the Nature and desire something different; you will fail to achieve what you need. Nature never likes a state of dilemma. Make it a habit to demand or ask from the Nature. But don't ask for a particular thing, again and again. You just have to ask one object only once from Nature. After that you have to assert yourself that particular demand must be fulfilled and you have achieved it.

You may have no money as of now. But you will have to develop the habit of feeling rich. You have to practice feeling rich for the conditions to become rich.

Whenever you make a demand from Nature, make a firm belief that you will definitely get it and convey thanks to Nature that you have achieved the goal. Nature with its full force will help you achieve what you want.

Faith is the assurance of things hoped for, the conviction of things not seen. Faith is to believe what you do not see; the reward of this faith is to see what you believe.

If you ever think with shattered thoughts- “I had not received in the past and may also not receive again this time.” This negative thinking will not let you gain.

For example, if you intend to go for a holiday, you confirm your hotels and tickets for the journey in advance. Looking at it won’t make a booking of another hotel or aeroplane for the same day for the simple reason that you have already confirmed it. Similarly when you are expecting the share of a property, you just assert yourself that you have got it! It is now that you enjoy the expressions of happiness.

The only reason you think negative is because you choose to do so. It has become your nature to think negative. You may have reached a state wherein you may find an excuse or another to feel negative. The same is true for happiness. The only reason you are happy is because you choose to be happy. Positive thoughts are chosen, so are negative thoughts.

If you want to be happy no one in this world can take happiness away from you; if you want to be unhappy, no one in this world can make you happy. So choose to be happy. It’s the faith in self that helps you. It’s the faith in Nature that helps you. Faith isn’t a feeling, it’s a choice to trust Nature, even when the road ahead seems uncertain.

Be innocent like a child and develop faith in Nature. Belief and faith are the most powerful forces in the Universe.

Nature has no phone, but you can talk to it. It has no facebook, but it is still your friend. It does not have twitter, but it still follows you. Sleep in peace tonight, Nature is bigger than anything you will witness tomorrow. Ask for, then let it go. Make a wish then visualize the happiness of owing it. Desire something, then feel, it is already yours. Do not try to manipulate or force the outcome. Just trust the Nature; it shall deliver you, at your door step, your choice at the right time.

From the moment you desire something, start believing that your wish has been fulfilled and be prepared to enjoy the miracles of Nature. Just don't think how these wishes and desires will be fulfilled! Nature will make arrangement of its own.

Sometimes when our beliefs are shaky, our desires are not fulfilled in time and we become sad and disgusted, our faith starts dwindling and we fall in distress. Don't fall in this trap, rather reaffirm yourself and make auto suggestions, "I know my desire is going to be materialized. I will achieve my goals. Have full faith in Nature." **Simply focus on the outcome, and let the universe complete its task. Faith is trusting, even when you don't understand the plan.**

❒

Chapter-3

Power of "Self Confidence"

At the time when you enjoy, you are connected with a chord of desires filled with happiness. Come on! let us feel, how happy we are! visualize that all your desires have been fulfilled! Say firmly that I am rejoiced like anything, so that everybody should feel the rejuvenation.

As long as you don't arouse the faith in yourself, don't ignite the lamp of love and don't feel the Nature, you can't awaken the powers of Universe. Try to feel the powers of Nature by arousing faith in yourself. You will feel the results of all these miracles provided you keep yourself full of joy, and believe me, all your desires would be fulfilled.

Self confidence is directly proportional to self belief i.e more the self belief more is the confidence and less of it will obviously lessen the confidence. Success automatically gets attracted to people with high self belief. Believe in yourself, have faith in your abilities. Without a reasonable confidence in your own powers, you cannot be successful or happy.

There is an immense strength in belief. With firm belief you ask for anything from nature, and it will be in front of you, without any delay.

Why do you gaze at the last step of the ladder? Just climb up the first step with firm belief and keep climbing one by one; the target will be in front of you.

Chapter-18, Shloka-66 from Shrimad Bhagavad Geeta, Lord Krishna says:

सर्वधर्मान्परित्यज्य मामेकं शरणं व्रज।
अहं त्वां सर्वपापेभ्यो मोक्षयिष्यामि मा शुचः ।। 66 ।।

Abandon all thoughts & faiths and just surrender unto Me. Leave fear, I shall free you from all sinful deeds..

When you take your food, concentrate yourself on eating. Chew it again and again, don't swallow it. You must have seen people running to office in car, driving with one hand, and swallowing food with the other hand. They are insulting Nature and annoying it. They are simply preparing to lose what they already have.

Enjoy the food. The more you chew, the more your relish it, and you enjoy with satisfaction. Also the taste of the food will increase manifold and your weight will remain in control.

You may enquire how much time it will take to fulfill the demands? when will I get the vehicle? when will I get a job? when will the children get the suitable match? There is no such law of Nature which defines how much time it will take! Three hours! Three days! or Thirty days! It can't be predicted. It all depends upon you how near you are to Nature and how much faith you have in it.

The most important thing for success is self belief and confidence. Believing that you deserve it, believing that you can do it, will certainly make you do it. Don't be pushed around by fears in your mind. Be led by the dreams in your heart. **A bird sitting on a tree is never afraid of the branch breaking; because her trust is not on the branch but on its own wings.**

Nature, offers you with open-hands and never stops giving out! Nature has already showered upon you what you desired/needed, but sometimes we fail to realize or feel it. At certain times it may be true that despite efforts and faith, you haven't got what you think you deserve. In such a case you need to thank you Karma for escaping now than at any later stage, accept it with grace and not let any incident shatter your faith in Nature.

Big or small is no consideration for Nature. There is nothing like hard for Nature. Everything is easy for Nature. The grass grows without putting any seed and without being cultivated by any person. There is no agitated effort in nature. The universe is formed in this way.

You throw any object as high as you can, earth will pull it down without exerting any efforts; because it is gravitational force of the earth which is effortlessly attracting everything towards itself. Similarly, the Nature is always in the habit of giving without identifying big or small.

You must have done a practical in junior classes about Guinea and Feather apparatus experiment, that earth attracts Guinea and Feather with equal gravitation, but it is the atmospheric obstruction which makes a difference between their falls. The Guinea and Feather is one of the most important experiments in classical physics and it is still performed today as a lecture demonstration for thousands of introductory physics students. It shows that the Earth's gravity accelerates all objects equally, regardless of mass i.e. a heavy object (a British Guinea) and a light object (a feather) will fall at exactly the same rate. The concept of uniform gravitational acceleration was proposed by Galileo Galilei (1564-1642). And later on confirmed by Isasac Newton in (1643-1727) mathematically as well as by this Guinea and Feather experiment in vacuum glass tube. Similarly

Nature does not differentiate between Re. 1 and Rs. 1 lac. It is the strength or weakness of your faith in Nature which can delay for long or deliver it at once. You think of drinking coffee, simply float the thought in the Nature and the coffee will be at your table. Think of the person whom you have not met for years, either he will be at your door step or his letter or phone call or text will be received by you.

Those who will be lucky are those who have faith in Nature. They make their lives according to their choice, because of their firm faith in the powers of Nature.

If you believe you can, you probably can. If you believe you won't, you most assuredly won't. **Belief is the ignition switch that gets you off the launching pad.** A leap of faith is not a plunge into darkness, but a dive into the light that others can't see.

The universe doesn't reflect what you say, it reflects what you feel. This is why reciting affirmations doesn't work to change your reality, unless you genuinely feel like those affirmations are true.

The way you chalk out the programme for the whole day early in the morning, similarly you can make your life in advance as well. When you get up in the morning make an auto suggestion that I am going on a beautiful journey or a positive mission. By doing this you are sending or floating the most important message in Nature and in reward the Nature will make your journey pleasant. If before going to shopping or any journey you spoil your mood, put yourself to irritation or curse yourself, it means you are sending wrong messages to Nature and Nature will let you face the same. **It is only your thought process, which makes both kind of situations; good or bad.**

The strongest factor for success is self-esteem and how exactly does self esteem rises? When we know whatever we are doing is actually right? When we know for the fact that our heart and mind are in balance. That in any circumstance, we are not going to stop believing in the goodness of life. That in any circumstances, we will not allow our-selfs to get bitter & bitter.

******

Life Changing benefits of* Gratitude *Practice

- ***Elevates your Mood***
- ***Increases your Energy***
- ***Improves your Health***
- ***Increases your Patience***
- ***Increases your Optimism***
- ***Improves your Relationships***
- ***Increases the power of Resiliency***
- ***Makes You Happier***

******

❐

Chapter-4

Negative Thoughts - Hurdles in Achievement

It starts just as a thought or a feeling, or may be as a sentence spoken by someone else; and then it starts to drag you down into feeling sorry for yourself, worried or auto suggesting yourself not to take any action. You walk around disdained. Negativity can quickly become toxic and hold you back.

Whenever you have to go somewhere and you are in haste, you remain in a state of stress that what if I get late? By putting this negative thought in Nature, you are creating obstructions one after another. It is you who is creating the trouble. This consistent restlessness agitation, confusion is not accepted by nature and what you get is further restlessness, agitation and confusion.

You would often find people saying, "I don't have time!" It means you are sending a message to Nature that you don't have time and as a result you actually start spoiling and wasting time. Rather you should say, 'I have lot of time' and your life will start changing for betterment.

Sometimes you have to wait; when you go to the Doctor, Railway Station, Airport, etc. You can utilize this time also. Think positive & keep yourself in a happy mood.

When you are in a clinic, you assume you are parting away your sickness or disease at Doctor's place. When you are waiting and feeling tired at Railway Station or Airport you should assume that you are enjoying a picnic or fiesta. By enjoying the situation, you are sending positive waves to Nature. With this little change in the thinking pattern, you can change the whole environment in a positive way & change even the adverse & opposite circumstances in your favour. To snap out of that put your attention fully into this moment, and into what's here right now.

Start making it a habit to spend more of your time in the present moment and you will, naturally have less negative thoughts and be more open and constructive.

Make a resolution that when you go to bed, chalk out the schedule for the next day and when you get up in the morning you will repeat the same programme, which you had planned out at night before sleeping. Now you have clear thoughts and clear programs for the whole day. These are not merely thoughts but messages to Nature which will start accomplishing your jobs and start paving a way for you in advance. As a result you decide and make the day as per your desire.

If you want to change your condition and environment you have to change your entire thought process. For example whenever you receive envelopes by courier unknowingly you say it might be bills. Nature can't disappoint you. You thought of bills, so nature did not betray you. It provided you your long pending bills.

Desire is power & hope is energy. Since it attracts everything towards itself, your will-power attract you to things you desire. Hence you should wish only those things which you desire. Think only positive, don't say, 'I do not want'. Say, 'I want this' or 'I want that'. It will come to you with a blink of an eye. The subconscious mind does not understand the language of 'don't, not or no.' So when you say, 'I don't want to meet this person/situation'. Nature takes it as 'I WANT to meet this person/situation.' So be very careful with your words/thoughts.

Frustrated people often say 'I am like this' only. If they peep into themselves, they would realize that they were not like this. They might have been jolly, adventurous, and harmonious. It is only because of their negative thoughts, that they are facing lack of money, indifferent health & tense relationships. One can come out of these difficult situations or adversities very easily. You only have to throw out the rotten thinking and negative thoughts from your mind.

Always remember, "One tree can make one lakh matchsticks, but one matchstick can burn one lakh trees." One negative thought in the morning can change the entire out come of your day. Say "I can" instead of "I Can't" and smile more often be optimistic and remember you are incharge of your thoughts. Change the thoughts and believe me, you can change your world. Your positive thoughts are both the prayers and answers to your prayers.

Always sprinkle your mind with new encouraging thoughts and positive thinking, send waves of fragrance to Nature. It will reward you forcefully, your future will start flourishing with new heights of progress and achievements.

You don't have to pray to attract great things, because great things are attracted to you already. Pray that you won't throw them away once they get to you.

******

When you are tapping into the negative thoughts then you are often thinking pattern about something that happened or something that might happen or both, all jumbled up, causing your mood and thoughts to sink.

To snap out of that put your attention fully into this moment, and into what's here right now.

******

******

Gratitude will turn every lack in your life into abundance, every sadness into happiness, every confusion into clarity and this being grateful will turn your dreams into reality….

Pt. Gopal Sharma

******

******

There is nothing lost in giving thanks,
a lot is gained and there is nothing
gained in complaining, rather a lot is lost.

******

❐

Chapter-5

Power of Gratitude

Gratitude is the healthiest of all human emotions. The more you express for what you have, the more likely it is that you will get even more. Gratitude Multiples.

Being grateful to Nature endorses the power within you. Start making a list of blessings for which you are thankful. As you sit down thoughtfully to make the list, you will be surprised at the blessing you have ignored so far. As you begin the list, you may start with

'I can see. I am thankful to my eyes.'

'I can walk. I am thankful for having a healthy body.'

'I have a car. I am thankful for the fact that I can travel in rains, in summers, in winters without much discomfort.

'I have parents. So many children are abandoned or orphaned.'

Each individuals comes from a different space & likewise each individual will have his/her own list to look forward to.

Reflect upon your present blessings, lat the past make noise. Don't hear the screams. It happens to many.

Generally, we concentrate on those things which we do not have or with which we have grudges or complaints. We are mostly attracted towards negative thoughts. We should withdraw our power of thoughts from negativity and should explore on those subjects or matters which give us happiness and make us delightful.

We are often caught up in our destination that we forget to appreciate the journey, especially the gifts received from the nature on the way. Gratitude is a special feeling don't overlook it.

We should always offer our sincere gratitude to the almighty, for this benevolence. Thoughts of thanks to the almighty, do not merely mingle with the Nature, rather they add to the power and happiness within us. Just think and realize how much you have gained by thanking the Almighty!

A "Thank You" will remove all your shortcomings and fill your life with happiness. If a wife honours and appreciates the small acts or favours done to her by her husband; he will naturally look forward to doing more obligations to her. Similarly, if the husband, feels grateful towards his wife, she will also return in abundance.

Similarly when you praise or thank others for minor things, you will feel that this act starts attracting support and love of others. When you get up in the morning, be grateful and convey thanks to the Almighty.

In Vedas it is very well elaborated as under:-

कराग्रे वसते लक्ष्मीः करमध्ये सरस्वती।
करमूले स्थितो ब्रहमस प्रभात करदर्शनम्॥

It means when you get up in the morning, first of all watch your palms and pray "The front portion of my palm is blessed with Goddess Lakshmi, the central part by Goddess Sarswati and in the roots of palms resides Brahma ji."

This is "Giving thanks" to the hand which brings earnings for us.

Similarly before putting your feet on the Mother Earth, you should pray or thank her by reciting the following Mantras.

समुद्रवसने देवि पर्वतस्तनमण्डिते।
विष्णु नमस्तुभ्यं पादस्पर्शं क्षमस्व मे।।

"Goddess Earth who is wearing Seas as her clothes and Mountains as her breast, who is better half of God Vishnu ji, please forgive me that I am putting feet upon you."

In the same way we can also express our gratitude to other forces of nature i.e. Wind, Water, Fire and Space.

You will soon realize that these prayers and thanks can shower immense blessings and happiness upon you.

The more you thank the universe, the more it will offer you. You should not thank God through mere words rather you should feel it within in your inner self.

By thanking the almighty, you gain energy from nature and make your day auspicious and favourable. This way you can easily control your day as per your wishes, since there is no other way except being grateful to Nature. Gratitude is a powerful process for shifting your energy and bringing more of what you want into your life.

A beautiful heart is one that is filled with gratitude and appreciation. A humble heart is the wellspring of great growth and development.

The poor people are passing through poverty for the simple reason that they don't float the word 'THANKS'. Float the words THANKS in the Nature for miraculous results.

If you aspire anything in your life, it can't be achieved without Thanks. If you lack something in your life, it is for the simple reason that you are not used to convey Thanks; rather you are desperate and ungrateful to Nature. The thoughts of pessimism and thanklessness arise due to jealousy, humiliation and insufficiency. Owing to these negative thoughts, you fail to achieve what you desire.

The reason why people do not have what they want is because they are thinking more about what they don't have, than what they do want. Analyze the thoughts and words you are saying. The law is absolute and nature does not make any mistakes.

First of all you "Feel Grateful" to the Nature for the things it has already provided you, keep on thanking and new positive thoughts will start cropping up. As soon as you start thanking, Nature will start sending you new thoughts and new goods to you, for which you may convey more thanks to Nature. By practising 'Thanks' daily to Nature you will gain the wealth that is in abundance in Nature. You will achieve wealth of Love, wealth of Health, wealth of wisdom, wealth of Money and whatever else you want.

Of course, there will be unfavourable times, times that will seem to be beyond your control, times that will test your patience. It is specially in those tiring time that you need to be mindful and not forget the law of Nature.

If you do not practice Gratitude, its benefactions will go unnoticed, and your capacity to draw on the gifts from Nature will be diminished.

To be grateful is to find blessings in everything. This is the most powerful attitude to adapt to, for there are really blessings in everything, but we fail to appreciate.

Gratitude turns denials into acceptance, chaos into order, confusion into clarity. It turns problems into gifts, failures into success, mistakes into blissful events. Gratitude heals the past, brings peace today and creates a vision for tomorrow.

❐

Chapter-6

Power of Imagination

For those who do not understand it, they call it Magic. But that's how the law of Nature is Call it Magic, Sciencc or faith; it has it own powers. Right imagination clubbed with good karma, faith & trust in the universe can being life altering experiences.

Late Dr. Sarvepalli Radhakrishnan, Former President of India, once well said that, *"Losers always think of the punishment, while the winners have the habit of always visualizing the prize & celebrations after victory."*

If you desire a car, you should not only assume that you are in a car, rather you should assert yourself that you are in a car driving and enjoying the highways and hills you are passing through.

Never say, if I were a car owner! Had the car been mine! Don't arouse an iota of doubt in your mind regarding the power of nature. Never say how can it be possible ? Or it is impossible! We cannot fathom the power of the universe; make a belief in yourself that this power will certainly help you to achieve anything you consistently strive for.

Nature knows the shortest way, least time consuming and the easiest path between you and your dreams. If you surrender yourself to this power of Almighty, you will be stunned to achieve miraculous results from nature. Your desires will be fulfilled in such a beautiful way that you will be amazingly surprised.

In Shrimad Bhagavad Geeta Lord Shri Krishna has testified in 35th shloka (Verse) of 9th Adhyay (Chapter):

मन्मना भव मद्भक्तो मद्याजी मां नमस्कुरु।
मामेवैष्यसि युक्त्वैवमात्मानं मत्परायणः॥

Engage your mind always in thinking of Me (Nature/God), become my devotee, offer obeisance to Me and worship Me. Being completely absorbed in Me, surely you will come to me.(Certainly you will achieve whatever you aspire).

Nature can do your entire task in blink of an eye. It always rewards the sincere dedicated efforts in right direction. Give you 100 percent for a purpose and keep this process of imagination continuously alive in your mind. The more you feel happy and confident, more your desires will be fulfilled with least efforts.

When you understand the law of nature, then you will realize that everything you imagine, good or bad, will infact come to you and that's just the unfailing simple law of Nature. Nature will bestow upon you the actions you need to take, the right decisions that you need to make, the right mind set that you need to have so as to fulfill your dreams.

Therefore it is said as soon as any doubt arises in your mind, thrash it away and say with confidence- "I am feeling the energy of Nature, my desires are going to be fulfilled, I am in complete harmony with Nature, with strong faith that all my desires have been fulfilled."

Imagination is the beginning of creation. The Wright Brothers imagined flying in the air and hence they created an aeroplane. Mother Teresa imagine giving a life of dignity to the poor and hence so many people were benefitted. Newton imagine that there could be something call 'light' in darkness and hence electricity was invented. It is simple. You have to imagine first.

You imagine what you desire. The world is a canvas of your imagination. You are the painter & there are no predetermined rules to paint it; you can paint it as per your desire.

Once upon a time, there was a businessman in Mumbai. He used to imagine a house of his dreams; and used to scribble the drawing of the house and car of his choice on the paper. Days and years went on passing. He changed three houses during a period of five years. Ultimately he owned a house and got it renovated and decorated according to his choice. One day his son came to his office and started searching some boxes lying in the office. These boxcs were having those drawings of the house which he had sketched down. When the businessman saw those papers he was stunned and started crying with tears in his eyes that his house was the same as he has dreamt. This is the power of Nature.

Just think what you need today and make it a belief that you will definitely get it. Be assertive that you are the rightful owner of the same and close your eyes for a minute and assume that you have achieved what you wanted. Now slowly open your eyes and come out of the dream and concentrate on the article or desire which have been fulfilled for which you are thankful to the universe.

Negative imagination is the No.1 root cause of self induced suffering. It becomes a pattern to imagine negative incidents that haven't even occurred. What happens when people watch negative news/TV series? They are literally on a look out for something negative that might happen to them which eventually turns into suffering/unwanted happening. When you are excited about something, you are using your power of imagination positively. By imagining the best, you are attracting the best to you.

Start your routine work by sowing the seeds of desires and thoughts in nature. Leave rest to the Nature and believe that it will be accomplished soon. Make it your daily habit to think in this fashion. This has to be done in a continuous fashion. All the worries will vanish away and you will achieve very easily whatever you want. Before going to bed, revise daily activities of the day. Think what you have done today, and what has been done knowingly by you. Avoid any negative thoughts being sent to Nature and make it a point to send only those positive thoughts to Nature, which you actually want.

Worry is a total waste of time. It doesn't change anything. All it does is to stop your joy and keep you very busy doing nothing. Worry is a form of imagination, but why worry if it attracts failure. Let imagination be positive, as it has the power to change your inner state and your outer world.

If you need money, then concentrate only on money and visualize spending it for your cherished dreams; if you need property then concentrate on enjoying the benefits of having that property.

In case you think that you do not have sufficient money then you are sending negative thoughts in the Nature, that you lack money; and the condition will start deteriorating. Rather start sending new messages to the nature that "I have money more than necessity and needs." For attracting wealth you will have to make an firm imagination that you have an abundance of money and put yourself into a happy and joyous mood; as you are enjoying the finances. Soon you will start feeling that you are actually getting the money and enjoying it.

You will soon realize that your worries about finance had started vanishing and happiness of having lots of money is being felt by you. When you start feeling this way in your life, the money will start coming by greater intensity and you will be surprised to experience the power of your positive thoughts.

As you achieve a certain state of calm, the forces in the universe will unite to bless you, what you need. If in restlessness, you keep trying to catch a butterfly, you will never be able to catch it. But if you are in a meditative state of mind, the butterfly may a come and sit on you shoulder.

For the forces of the universe to work in the betterment of you, you need to at least in a receiving state.

To stop negative thinking does not mean not seen negative as negative. No! For example if a person is evil and does not mean right to you, then you need to maintain a certain distance from that person. Herein, when we talk about coming out of negative thinking in terms of coming out of the 'worry' pattern; which is self induced suffering.

The more positive energy you have around you, the better you will feel about yourself.

Success is all about faith and the power of imagination to sustain faith. It's all about the desire to feel happy.

"THINK IT, BELIEVE IT & RECEIVE IT"

******

"Thank you" is the key to a healthier and happier life, which helps us to enjoy every moment of the day.

******

❒

Chapter-7

Fulfilment of Desires by Nature

Our ancient Rishis(saints) have summarized the philosophy of whole universe in the Upnishada's. According to the first Shloka of Ishwashy Upnishad.

ॐ पूर्णमदः पूर्णमिदं पूर्णात्पूर्णमुदच्यते ।
पूर्णस्य पूर्णमादाय पूर्णमेवावशिष्यते ।।

It means: "The nature or the universe is complete in itself. Only the complete can produce the complete. If you withdraw the complete out of the complete, the remainder will also be complete in itself."

So it is self evident that Nature is complete and perfect, and we can take out of it as much as we want to and still there will be no dearth or scarcity in Universe.

Close your eyes and visualize having what you really want and the feeling of having it already. Focus on being grateful for what you have already and enjoy it, then release into the universe; which will manifest it in no time.

You can sign a cheque of any amount in your name from Nature. Fill up all your details and the amount you seek. Paste it at a place where you can notice it daily. Whenever you see this cheque you can make yourself believe that this is your own amount and also feel that you are spending it for your needs and buy whatever you want to buy. You assume that you are purchasing all those things and feel the happiness and joy of purchasing.

The only reason that people do not have a sufficient amount and amenities with them is that they always think of shortage and lack of money. These thoughts and negative waves are sent to Nature and it eventually withholds the way of their progress. Actually it is not any body else, but it is they who are the culprits, by emitting negative waves to the Nature.

There is abundance of money but it is not visible. If anybody is stopping money to come to you, it is waves you own pessimistic thoughts sent to Nature, which are creating the obstructions in your progress and development. Instead of concentrating on shortage or lack of money, concentrate your thoughts on the abundance and collecting and owning immense money. You will feel that you are enjoying happiness and all kinds of fulfillment. Keep on thinking positive, and big. Flush out the thought of shortage and go on increasing the thought of abundance. If you think of accumulating money you are sending a powerful and positive thought to the Nature. Nature will automatically accept the thoughts of your necessity and will fulfill your desires. From this very moment start feeling happy and joyful. This is the best way to attract money for yourself from nature.

Ask once, and start believing that you have received. Nature's law says that all you have to do to receive is, to feel good. When you feel good/happy you are on the frequency of receiving. You are on the frequency of all good things coming to you, and you will certainly receive what you have asked for.

The moment you send thoughts of happiness and joy to nature, positive waves will be sent to you by nature. The kind of waves you send to Nature, comes back to you; just as every action has an equal and opposite reaction.

The Nature can't bring you what you want just because you want it. You have to be a match to it; your thoughts, your feelings, belief and your karmas should be in harmony to bring it into your life.

What you think you become, what you feel you attract, what you imagine you create, you are your own desires; as is your desire so is your will, as is your will so is your effort and as is your effort, so is your destiny.

If someone doubts HOW can he get money, while he is simply in a job? he is sending negative waves to the Universe. Never say "How" to Nature. It does not like doubts. Just say that you need this much or that much. Suppose you need Rs. One million, just send this message to Nature and start waiting with full faith and confidence.

If you are thinking, 'how' will you get money from your job, then remove this thought from your mind. You are concerned with money only. How it will come to you is the job of Universe. It is the duty of Nature to provide it to you. You just feel that you are getting it and leave rest to Nature. You will be surprised that your desire have been fulfilled. Believe in what you want so much that it has no choice but to materialize.

Some people say our main aim is to get rid of loan and debt. This thought is specified with the word debt. Since this word 'Debt' is sent to Nature, it will reciprocately keep him indulged in debts and loans, because he is thinking of loans and debts alone. It is not a matter of indulging or getting rid of loans. It is a thought of loan itself. Just make an instalment of loan and start paying back the debts and keep thinking of more money and happiness of living in Abundance.

There is sometimes delay when you think about something and the time it takes to come to you. This delay as an opportunity to focus your attention more and more on what you really want to achieve in your life. It's not Nature who is responsible for this debacle, but it is you yourself who is sending negative currents in the Universe.

"Believe and conceive; the life you perceive is the life you will receive. Have faith in every act of Nature while you learn how to wait. Eventually you will receive a gift that is great."

You can create anything you want, but to do that you must follow the Law of Nature. Eliminate all doubt and replace it with full expectation that you will receive what you are asking for. If you are not receiving what you are asking, it's not Nature that has failed; it only means that your doubt is greater than your faith.

******

Think creatively!!

Think and dream creatively. Believe that it can be done and the mind finds way to get it done.

******

❒

Chapter-8

Power of Aspiration

People are often found uttering these words, "I can't buy this" or "I can't buy that!" You will have to; for your own good; stop uttering these words. Instead of saying, "I can't buy," say affirmatively, "I CAN buy it." Keep it repeating like a parrot. From now onwards whatever you see or whichever item comes across you, you just repeat 'I can buy it; I will buy it.' If you happen to see beautiful jewellery or car; just give an auto suggestion to yourself 'I CAN buy it.' I am going to get it.

Just by repeating these words you will feel a positive change in yourself. Financially you will grow stronger and stronger. And you will realize that you can purchase anything which you desire. Whenever you continue to think of scarcity or lack of anything, you are bound to fall in distress and a state of sorrowness.

Lord Krishna has very well defined in Shrimad Bhagavad Gita, in Shloka (Verse) No. 62 & 63 of Adhayaya (Chapter) 2:-

ध्यायतो विषयान्पुंसः सङ्गस्तेषूपजायते ।
सङ्गात्सञ्जायते कामः कामात्क्रोधोऽभियाते ।। 62 ।।

क्रोधाद्भवति सम्मोहः सम्मोहात्स्मृतिविभ्रमः ।
स्मृतिभ्रंशाद्बुद्धिनाशो बुद्धिनाशात्प्रणश्यति ।। 62 ।।

Thinking of objects of the sense,
A man for them attachment forms,
from attachment comes desire
And anger from desire is born.
From anger doth delusion rise,
And from delusion is memory's loss.
From memory's loss is wisdom's death,
with wisdom's death, he perishes.

If you discuss or involve yourself in scarcity with your family members, friends or children, it means you are weaving a web of adversity and scarcity around yourself, your family members, friends and children as well.

If you keep on mentioning what you do not have or that you are facing shortage, then you will fail to attain anything and will not be capable to achieve or purchase anything worth while in your life.

If you desire harmony, happiness and progress then also you will have to follow the same positive traits. All your thoughts should be concentrated upon growth and progress only.

Nature has unending heaps of wealth. If you come across a rich man it is because he has never let an idea of poverty or scarcity enter his mind.

Rich people sow the seed of growth, wealth and progress in Nature; and in return Nature rewards them with wealth and happiness. The wealth is also aspiring to embrace you; provided you are receptive to it. Wealth is waiting for you, it is ready to come to you. You just have to aspire and invite it.

Many people who have already started this practice, have started receiving huge sums into their accounts. It's because they had already sown the seeds of growth in the Nature.

There was a man who kept failing in wrong relationships. Women always left him. He was left with nothing but low self esteem. For almost five years, he was completely heartbroken, preciously because he kept, concentrating on negative stories around him. Stories that crystallized his belief that relationship don't work.

As his consciousness grew, he started working on himself and started practicing positive beliefs about relationship. As he worked on himself, his self esteem also grew. And it was then that he attracted a sustainable relationship for himself.

In past, if you were used to saying, "I earn money with great hardship," now start saying, "I am getting money instantly, easily and more than my needs."

Believe me, your life will change. Thousands of people, across the globe have already benefitted with this simple yet effective technique.

In the beginning it may look a farce & your brain and heart may not agree, but just keep practicing and throw away all the negative thoughts. Money will soon start coming easily, quickly and in abundance.

If you need wealth just keep asserting with faith that

- I have more wealth than what I need.
- I am enjoying happiness and prosperity.
- Wealth is flowing towards me and I am enjoying happiness.
- I love wealth and wealth loves me.
- Money is showering upon me daily.
- Many many many thanks to Nature.
- Charity is a Great Power.

Charity is indeed the biggest power to attract money. Always say, 'I have plenty of wealth.' You must be aware of the fact that richest people are philanthropists. They donate maximum part of their wealth in charity, and as per the Law of Nature it returns to them manifold. Nature gives them more and more and they always live in abundance.

When you think or say, 'I do not have sufficient money to donate,' it means you are caught wrong footed. You must realize this blunder. It is the reaction of this thought that you are facing scarcity of money.

When you feel that you have scarcity of money, then you should start donating some part of it. Slowly and steadily your faith will be established in Nature, that as you donate money, more wealth starts pouring upon you for charity purposes. You might have realized and wondered how people are continuously donating money in religious places such as Temples, Gurudwaras, Churches and Mosques. It is because of the simple reason that the person who donates more, gets more and more from the Nature or God. This is the miracle of Charity.

There is an eternal truth that there are three states of wealth:

- Charity/Donation.
- Self Use/Enjoyment
- Destruction.

As Lord Shri Krishna gives sermon to Arjuna in Shrimad Bhagavad Gita in third Adhyay in 11th and 12th Shlokas:

देवान्भावयतानेन ते देवा भावयन्तु वः।
परस्परं भावयन्तः श्रेयः परमवाप्स्यथ ।। अ.3 श्लोक 11

इष्टान्भोगान्हि वो दास्यन्ते यज्ञभाविताः।
तैर्दत्तानप्रदायैभ्यो भुंक्ते स्तेन एव सः ।। अ.3 श्लोक 12

It means "The demigods (Nature), being pleased by sacrifices, will also please you. and thus. by cooperation between men and demigods (Universe), prosperity will reign for all.

In charge of the various necessities of life, the demigods, being satisfied by the performance of yajna (sacrifice), will supply all necessities to you. But he who enjoys such gifts without offering them to charity in return, is certainly a thief."

When you attain or gain money and do not take out the share for charity, it is certain that wealth is going to part ways with you. After earning money first of all you should take out the money for then you should use rest of the money for your needs. You should try to give maximum for the help of your relatives, friends and needy people. By such act of charity, you are sending positive waves in the Nature and Nature gives you more and more.

If you donate money or wealth willingly and gladly with open heart and hands, the Law of abundance in Nature will apply. The more you distribute the more will be showered upon you. When you are enjoying the donations with open heart you will find phenomenal financial success in business and unique happiness at home.

Great people say, "Those who keep on accumulating money for themselves and have no affinity, love and sympathy with others, they are known as Poor." This is because they do not have emotions of love and feelings of sympathy for others.

You should assume and feel that you are the Lord of universe. Accomplishment in all the fields is your birth right. You have a key of happiness in your hands. You are the rightful owner of all the good things existing in the world. Nature will fulfill all your wishes, provided you just give a call to it. The key of success and happiness lies in your process of thinking, achieving, distributing, charity & enjoyment.

People are struggling hard to achieve success. Usually for people, at large, the goal of success is to acquire a luxurious house and well paying business or job; but Eternal happiness can only be achieved through soul and not through these materialistic comforts. We keep on accumulating materialistic items with a view that these will provide us happiness and satisfaction; but this is not the right path. We have to look within ourselves to find the drop of eternal happiness.

Eternal satisfaction, eternal peace and eternal love are within ourselves and we have to realize them. Once we attain this goal, outwardly comforts will automatically follow. You should behave or treat other people, as you wish to be treated by others. It simply means, that if you seek respect or love from others you have to render same love and affection to others as well. Similarly if you wish to receive financial abundance from Nature, you have to be grateful to the universe, for the existing blessing in life & start donations/charity to the needy ones; from whatever you have.

You should maintain your own dignity and respect only then others will give you love, regard and respect. Doing so you will be changing the environment around you. Whatever you do, you should do with peaceful thoughts. When you treat yourself with commitment then you will earn respect and honour from others.

Soon you will start realizing that it's your behaviour and committed thoughts that has earned you regard and respect, which are reciprocal reflection of you. If there is any scarcity around, the fault is not of other peoples but it is yours. If you think of yourself as great and dignified, you will earn dignity. If you put yourself in a state of humiliation and in a depressed state, society will look upon you in the same way. It is the Law of Nature, which will let you meet with the type of persons, you desire.

Most of the people think that they should make charity, but any donation is not effective till it is done from the core of heart and without a sense of egoism.

Nature has everything in abundance for everybody. Each and every person can aspire and fulfill his desired expectations from Nature. You can seek from the Nature for yourself but not for others. Similarly your job is to be done by yourself and not by others. It is simply because you can change your thought process, which others can't do for you. Your thinking is absolutely original and your thoughts are basically what you are.

Do not remind others - "I have done this or that for you, now it's your turn. It's your duty to pay me back now." Have a great heart and courage to shower upon others, without any expectations/wish of return. Only then you will be full of materialistic things around. If you share love, submissiveness, wisdom & money with others, then it will automatically return back to you in abundance.

******

Focus on target!!

Charge yourself up. Energize your willpower, stay focused on your target and take steps. The race is between you and your attitude.

******

❒

Chapter-9

Evolution of Self-Respect

You are being taught from childhood that you should accept leftover or surplus things and keep yourself in the last. This thought process unknowingly creates a sense that you are a useless and unwanted person. From ancient times, this kind of thinking is packed in our thought process. As a result we get ourself attracted towards such circumstances which are known as a sacrifice and full of remorse. To love yourself and keep yourself in the front row and seek maximum love and respect for yourself is not at all a wrong notion. Always live like a number one or in forefront.

As long as you are not self-sufficient, you cannot make charity or donate to other people. So, first fill up your own coffers.

Right to enjoy in yourself is a feeling of eternal happiness. Happiness and joy should usher from your inner self; so that others may see the shine of joy on your face and they may also enjoy the bliss in your presence. When you are in a state of happiness you do not worry what you are giving to others. It overflows automatically from you.

We normally depend upon others for the appreciation of our beauty and beautiful habits to be seen and praised by them. We do not appreciate our beauty of our own.

First of all we should learn how to love our own self, only then others will start loving us. When we fail to appreciate ourself, it means we are denouncing the love which is floating in Nature.

When you do not know your own worth and value, then do not expect someone else to calculate it for you.

When you start assuming yourself as a low-lived, poor or useless person, it means you are killing your courage and favour from your inner soul. The person who loves and evaluates himself, attains healthy body, money, love and accomplishment in all fields. If you remain in a sullen mood and keep meeting such persons who are in a state of sadness and always convey their disappointing thoughts, then you will have no value of yourself.

Change yourself, think and try to find out the specialties and good things in yourself. Write down those qualities on the paper. More you search the qualities more you will find within yourself. You have to start appreciating yourself, and in a small time nature will start appreciating you in leaps and bounds.

There is nothing wrong when you say, "Something unique is in me, miracle is in me," this is not at all an arrogance or egoism. You will start seeing your true inner self. The one who loves self, others naturally start loving him.

We should rather be alone with dignity than in a relationship that requires us to sacrifice our self respect. We may lose the person whom we love but we choose something much better; self respect.

In case relations have become sour with a person and you would like to improve, then start jotting down his virtues, which you like. Repeat this process for thirty days. You may write all the positive aspects, like his act of laughing, making jokes, habit of care & concern; whatever you appreciate. Also write down the support he/she has rendered you in difficult times. Now you have to concentrate on the good acts and specialties, only. Soon you will start feeling how good is that person and the rift in relations will eventually subside.

Sometimes you offer some opportunity or help to another person, which gives you happiness in return. Though at times they may fail to meet your expectation; which may make you unhappy. Here you are the cause of unhappiness because you helped that person on expecting a favour and not with the mere joy of helping the person. Always remember that you yourself are responsible for your own happiness, enjoyment and accomplishment.

Sometimes the unexpected behaviour of your spouse, abusing parents, un-attending children, careless staff and non-cooperative boss, do bring distress/low self esteem. But you must always remember, that eternal happiness lies within yourself only.

Analyze the point to recognize if you are suffering from low self respect.

1) You tend to measure yourself by other people's standards.
2) You rarely find moments of joy, peace and satisfaction in your life.
3) You tell white lies to please others, even when your decision was right.
4) You usually do things to please other even if it makes you unhappy.
5) You are often angry, even small events can send you into a rage.
6) You place a greater value on the opinions of other people than on your own.
7) You have trouble letting go of things; that happened in the past.

8) You feel very uncomfortable asking other people for help.
9) You treat the people, who love you, poorly.
10) You hold grudges; even if they destroy relationships that used to be very meaningful to you.
11) You are very hard on yourself when you make a decision.
12) You prioritize well being of others; even strangers, over your own self care.
13) You find if difficult and hard to apologize for your behavior.
14) You often find yourself criticizing others, even if you later realize you had no reason to do so.
15) You judge others very harshly. Nobody seems to meet your high standards.

Happiness and joy are totally dependent on love, which is the most powerful force. You cannot hold love in your fist, it can only be felt in the heart; it is the state of mind. You can see the glimpse of love on the face of others. But you alone have the power to arouse or shower love upon others.

When you put or generate love and compassion in your heart towards someone, Nature is offering you an opportunity to make a difference in that person's life. You must learn to follow that love. Do not ignore it. Act on it. More you shower on others, Nature returns back in abundance. And you start to receive love and respect from others.

It is absolutely true that you have an immense power to arouse love in yourself. When you love others then you become one with Nature, the force of almighty God. It indirectly means that you have attained God; the ultimate source of love and happiness. Think and concentrate only upon those people whom you love and you will find that in reward you are getting love, happiness and eternal peace. Love is increasing manifold and nature is sending more and more love to you.

You need to understand that if you do not respect yourself, then no one will respect you.

Remember the world sees what you put out there, so hold yourself to a high standard of grace and elegance. Be a reflection of what you want to receive from Nature.

As you wear the robe of love you will feel that Nature is working for you. It is bringing everything, which can give you happiness. It is bringing all good people around you.

Self-respect is the single greatest commodity a person can own. With it, you can take on any challenge, bounce back from any fall, make everything go right. You know that you deserve the best, so go out and get it! You do not shy away from opportunities, you make them! You do not run away from love, you embrace it and make more!

Suddenly you stop being the effect and start being the cause over your own life; you now have control! You know who you are, you know where you are going, and you can say this with certainty because you know that when you make a decision and stick to it Nature returns back in abundance.

Happiness is a choice, not a result. Nothing will make you happy until you choose to be happy. No person will make you happy, unless you decide to be happy. Your happiness will not come to you; it can only come from you.

❐

Chapter-10

Importance of the Desire to be Healthy

As a matter of fact, our body is a structure of our thoughts and assumptions. Medical science has started accepting the fact that our thoughts cast an impact on our health. Most forceful power is our brain which keeps our body healthy.

When a patient develops a faith in his mind that he will be cured by a particular tablet, he becomes healthy by taking that tablet. Always consider yourself a healthy person, capable of enjoying every moment of life.

Nature is much more comprehensive than abundance. In Nature, everything is in abundant quantity. When you open your heart or surrender yourself before the Nature, then your inner self gets fulfilled with love, joy, happiness and with fervor. You can withdraw as much as you want from Nature like as good health, lots of money, good behaviour and any positive thing which you aspire. But if you develop sad and negative thoughts, it means you are separating yourself from Nature. You will become restless, the whole body starts paining, physically as well as mentally and each day would become difficult to pass.

There are millions of disease but thousands of cures are made for these diseases. There are certain weak links in our body. These are the growth of the single seed, which is known as stress. If you put a little stress on these weak links, more stress is generated within whole body. A single evil thought entering our thought process, if not deterred will bring another similar thought with it, till it makes a full chain of stress. We feel stress which is visible to us, but we fail to notice that this chain of stress was due to the growth of single evil thought. Stop thinking about what evil has happened in the past. You can change the process by thinking about good and positive events and replace bad and evil thoughts with them.

Whenever we fall sick, we should consider the fact that this is the indication of our inner self being in imbalanced state. We have lost the harmony between the love and ourself. Hence, this ill-health is not a bad omen rather a warning for us to remain in love and harmony with our body.

Padma Shri Dr. Randeep Guleria, AIIMS Delhi, once explained that expression of love and gratitude, expression of appreciation to Nature can ward away all the negativity from our lives. Love and gratitude can churn the sea and shake the mountains and can make many miracles. So love and harmony can cure any kind of diseases.

Somebody asked the question, 'If a disease has entered the temple of the body, restlessness bites it like termite.' 'Can his positive thoughts and optimistic thinking help him to recover from the disease?' He got an answer 'Yes, definitely he will recover.'

Once a lady fell victim to cancer, but mentally she was so strong that she strengthened her belief that she will cure herself from this disease. She daily used to repeat, 'Thank you God for curing me, I again thank you for recovering me.' Daily she used to think that, 'I have recovered,' she never considered herself to be a cancer patient. She used to laugh daily & enjoyed watching entertaining and comedy films to keep herself in delightful mood. She always used to say that she cannot allow stress to enter her mind, as it is the only ingredient which does not allow the person, to get cured.

It took her only three months to recover. Though it may seem as an unbelievable fact but she never underwent any kind of chemotherapy or radiotherapy or any kind of treatment. This true story of a girl named Swathi, reflects three forceful powers.

- First power is to convey 'Thanks' to 'Nature'.
- Second is the power of faith that 'I am Recovering'.
- Third power is 'To burst in laughter and to remain Happy and Joyful'.

These three miracles can keep all our diseases away from us.

Swathi says- it was his friend Vinod who gave her the inspiration to get herself cured. Earlier Vinod was also suffering from an incurable disease and the doctors had refused to treat him. They rather told him that he will survive only for a few months. Vinod made a pledge to himself that he has to cure himself and become healthy. Continuously for three months he enjoyed comedy films. While enjoying films he kept laughing, laughing and laughing. The disease left his body within three months. Doctors declared it as a miracle. As Vinod kept on laughing the pessimism kept running and melting away and the disease left him. The true fact is that laughing is the most effective medicine.

A body which does not suffer from mental stress can never suffer from a physical disease. It is medically proved that every moment million of cells are dying but millions are getting regenerated as well. As a result, practically new body parts are surging, though some parts may take months to grow and some may take years; but just visualize that in few years we get a new body. This way no disease can live within a body; forever. The disease lives in the body only because we think about it, or we keep a watch on it every moment or we give importance to it.

From now onwards, keep transcendent and happy thoughts in mind, disease can never enter your body and can never exist in it. You should nourish the mind with thoughts of love and harmony. Remember, Nature has everything in abundance and gives you in abundance. If you maintain the thought of accomplishment and excellence in your mind; then eventually you will get all those. Evil and biased thoughts are the root of diseases. Poverty, distress and sorrow arise due to evil and bad thoughts. When we start in a negative and pessimistic way, we keep ourselves away from all good rewards of Nature.

Let all people know and make an announcement loudly from the core of heart - 'I only have accomplished thoughts and see everything in the completeness. I am the best.' Let go off all the thoughts of egoism and nepotism from your heart. Think like a child, all pure thoughts, think actively and with a flexible mind. As you invite positive thoughts within yourself; the egoism, the pain, the rheumatic pains and laziness will evaporate from body. This is a tried, tested and trusted experiment. The one who does it can feel the miraculous effects.

We tend to believe that we are growing old. Whereas science has claimed that after every few years, our body keeps re-juvinating itself. Thinking of growing old is a pity thought; so remove it from your mind rather inner soul. Though you might have celebrated many birthdays, do a favour by celebrating your next birthday by simply burning a single candle.

If you want to make yourself young, do not light 60 candles. Just assume about yourself that you are free from disease, you are healthy, accomplished, having positive thoughts, proper weight and unending youth. This will give you eternal happiness and make you do much better in life.

If somebody is suffering from a disease and putting entire concentration on sickness and keeps on talking about it with friends and relatives, it means he or she is creating a permanent place in the body for the diseases. Shunt out these negative thoughts & throw them away. Consider yourself having a perfect healthy body and leave the rest on the doctor.

One thing is very common among people, when they fall sick, they talk about sickness all the time. This is because they have their entire focus on the disease. If you are feeling sick do not discuss about sickness. If you do not want to remain sick, you should clearly understand that your thinking process has brought sickness or disease in your body. So say again and again 'I am healthy and feeling very fine'. If somebody enquires about your health, reply him, 'I am perfectly fine.'

You cannot catch any article or a thing until you decide to catch it. But if you think that you will catch it, then you capture it, with your own thoughts. You invite disease, the moment you go to enquire the well being of others or listen to anybody talking about disease. You fully concentrate on the thought of disease, as a result you invite them. By listening and sympathizing with them you are helping them in no way. If you really want to help them, change the subject from disease to other healthy discussions.

It is imperative to know that you may come across one or more issues in life, may be in the matters of health, wealth or relationship. The point here is to have a right mind set, which will be of great help in solving the problems.

Now we are putting a step forward in a new era. This era is of 'Courage Power Medicine'. In the Nature every article has a signal. Change the signal to a good thought, as a results of which everything will be easy to change; it may be either health or profession or the matter of relationships. If you have the courage everything is easy for you.

Sometimes the best thing you can do is not to think, not to wonder, not to imagine, not to obsess. Just breathe freely, choose to be happy and have complete faith in Nature .

******

The loving invitation to live the life you desire,
is to know that the only obstacle which stands
between you and your well-being, is a simple fact: -
You have allowed your thoughts and emotions
to take instructions from outside, then inside.
Realizing this, Think, Act, Feel & receive,
anything, based on your desire;
creating the life you truly cherish.

******

❐

Chapter-11

Be Positive to be Happy!

Generally it is observed that when people look at a thing anywhere, either in the market or any other place, they are generally found saying, 'Yes I want this, I like it.' But the thing which they do not want and which they do not like they are often found saying, 'I don't want this, I don't like.' It means they emphasize upon both the things with same intensity. We keep on fighting with things which we dislike, such as fight against poverty to remove poverty, fight against terrorism and fight against violence. We are fighting for those things which we do not like. But as a matter of fact we are actually creating fight. We need to change this outlook, concentrate on ideas for wealth & creation and activities that generate peace.

If we concentrate on a thought, it means we are adding to its intensity. If you are in a state of anger due to some quarrel, it means you are flaring up the differences rather than pacifying it. To oppose a fight is to invite fight. Such as, if you oppose against drugs, it means you are attracting drugs. This indicates your entire concentration is upon fight and drugs. People often think, if we want to suppress something we should concentrate upon it. Is it a wise step, that we concentrate our energy on the matter which we want to finish? What you resist you persist so if you want something to stop you should stop concentrating on it, over and over again & look for a permanent solution.

Mother Teresa has quoted - *'I will not participate in any rally which is against war. But will take out the procession for peace. You may call me at any time.'* It means Mother Teresa had realized the power of thinking. If we fight for something the fight will be in front of us. You can see how Mother Teresa has given peace to the world.

Thinking good and positive is the first step towards better physical and mental well being. Positive thinking doesn't mean keeping your head in the sand and ignoring difficult situations. Thinking positive just means that you approach unpleasantness in a more positive and productive way.

Do not lead rallies against the war, but take out processions for peace. Rally should not be against poverty but for the sake of prosperity. If you want to fight against a leader then you should support a leader who is fighting against him. It's often found that a person who has maximum opposition, generally wins. It is for the simple reason that he gets the power of those who are opposing him.

Everything in the world starts with a seed of thought. If we remove our concentration from negativity and direct our focus on love and peace; anger, hatred & poverty will fade away.

If someone is facing any adversity or suffering from any disease, he may be far away from you, but if you constantly think about him, you may also become sick.

You must know what you aspire and to what extent you desire it. Otherwise how will you know what you want? Unfortunately we spend more time discussing those things or situations which we actually do not want.

Nature treats all your thoughts in the same manner. So, when you think or visualize about what you want or what you could be, you are giving Nature more information to work with. Your thoughts, opinions, behavior and choices will soon begin to follow suit and take your life in a more creative direction.

By listening to or thinking of bad ideas you are neither helping yourself nor the world, at large. If you are concentrating on negative or evil deeds happening in the world, it means you are filling yourself with negative thoughts and a sense of scarcity in your own life.

When you are inviting negative thoughts, nature listens to you and brings them in your life. But it is also a fact that no matter how hard you try, there are times when you just can't stop feeling negative about everything around you. The more you try to push these negative thoughts away, the more they will return with a vengeance.

What you focus on is what Nature gives you.

If there is any problem in the world, you should not feel helpless because you have immense powers. Just think and concentrate on betterment alone. Concentrate all your forceful thoughts upon all the things that you want in your life. You have a lot to give to the world. Let the ocean of love flow from yourself for the help of others, whatever it may be, let it happen around you.

If the company of a person or TV programs or newspaper and media is giving stress to you and you are still continuing with it, the fault is not that of the person or media's; it is your own blunder. Those bad deeds which are shown or printed, are sub-conciously created by us only. Whenever sensational news occurs you start running to buy papers or switch on the TV. If we listen about calamities on the news channel, the number of viewers increase manifold. Papers and TV channels add more stories to it as we demanded.

Try to be stable and remove your focus from the things that you do not like. For this you have to concentrate on your own self. Try to spend maximum time on concentrating on positive thoughts. Energy flows to the direction where the thought process moves. We are born to manifest the glory of God, that is within us. It's not just in some of us, it's in everyone.

I believe you are great; I believe there is something great about you, something magnificent about you. Regardless of what has happened in your life, regardless of how young or how old you think you might be; the moment you begin to think positive success begins to surface and Nature becomes your companion.

Stay positive, the things you are waiting and hoping for, tend to arrive at the most unexpected moments. There is a power and magic to whatever you are thinking. Positive thinking plants the seed for positive life experiences. Positive thinking will keep you optimistic and happy even during hard times. Positive thinking isn't about the best to happen every time, but accepting that whatever happens is indeed the best for that moment.

Our thoughts are our responsibility, and it's only when we accept the responsibility, we can change how we are experiencing life. We attract from Nature what we put out there. If we want to feel an abundant return of good energy, we must give with willingness first.

Happiness is here right now; in fact, it's never been any where else but here and it's yours.

"Happiness, not in another place, but this place; not for another hour, but this hour." Walt Whitman's words sound true, no matter where you are, who you are, or what you are experiencing.

There is enough happiness for everyone in Nature, the place of abundance. There is enough of everything enough money, enough time, enough love, enough praise, enough happiness, enough of everything that we need. The universe is not shrinking, and its our task and responsibility to align ourselves to the vastness of Nature.

Your mind is a powerful tool. When you fill it with positive thoughts, your life will start to change. This is the secret Law of Nature, it gives you more and more of what you desire.

A good life is when you assume nothing; do your karma-follow your dharma, smile often, dream big, laugh a lot, and realize how blessed you are for what you have.

******

All of us pass through a phase when we feel that all is not happening the way we desire, rather it is deteriorating. At this moment, we should not concentrate on those unfavourable objects or circumstances. Even in those moments we should be thankful for good things to Nature, and our life will start turning to a beautiful Future.

******

❐

Chapter-12

Key to Evolution

You are born in this universe for a special cause. You have a mission to accomplish. And to do so you have to be more positive and feel more energetic and rejuvenated. By this process you succeed in blossoming harmonious feelings in the atmosphere and in the entire universe. Doing this, you fill up your life with beauty and eternity. When you are in a state of happiness and joy then you are moving towards evolution. With this you are evolving the whole world around you as well.

When you start feeling that you are listening to the voice of your eternal soul then everything is very clear in spite of the noise. It means you have got victory over your senses and on yourself.

Your aim is to attune yourself with the flow of the universe; you have to swim with the current of the river, fly with the wind, and to rejuvenate yourself with the universe. You are the Lord of yourself and Nature is to obey your command. Make a web of new thoughts which are needed by you and feel that you are recharging yourself. Thank the Almighty that you refrained yourself from the unwanted things.

A single false statement can shake the entire humanity. People are suffering from scarcity, fear, miserliness and greed because of their limited beliefs. It seems as if the entire world has pledged itself to suffer from the sense of insecurity and scarcity.

The truth is that there is an abundance of everything for everyone at all times. There are unlimited number of arts, new inventions and discoveries in the universe. Nature is full of energy. All of this comes from a single brain; from the brain which has immense energy and clarity of thoughts and ideas in it.

If you look at the universe outwardly you would find scarcity and a lack of everything. But nothing comes from outside, everything is within yourself. Everything begins or emerges from a thought in a brain. You can produce in the brain as much as you need. Then there will not be scarcity of anything.

Your power of thinking is unlimited and beyond any boundaries. Similarly everybody has limitless power to think. When you accept this fact from the core of your heart then your brain will start working accordingly and you will be able to increase the energy and power of your brain. Great many people have proved that there is no scarcity in Nature. Everything is in abundance.

As soon as anything is about to be consumed, better will take its place and will serve the same purpose. There is nothing limited, neither the ways nor means; neither the articles nor the things. If there is any scarcity that is only in our brains. If you think with open heart and open mind you will always find complete perfection and abundance in nature. We are born in this beautiful world and we are infested with the power of beautiful thoughts. There is no limitations to produce anything by mere assumption. You cannot thrust or impose your thoughts upon others. So let others live the way they like. Let them take their own decisions.

In case you are suffering due to poverty, scarcity or disease, it is for the simple reason that you are rigid in not changing your belief system. Nature has given this power not only to you but to everybody and is ready to offer it in equality to everyone. You must learn the art of inviting unlimited power of the abundance. This is a unique and wonderful view. Nature is at your command; it's only you who choose good or bad for yourself.

When you wish good for others good things surround you with their beauty, this is the Law of Nature.

Whatever you want such as love, happiness, satisfaction and fulfilment; this is already for you in the Nature. You have to think and grab it. You have to do it intentionally and knowingly. When your heart burns with an aspiration for these things then Nature will automatically shower love, happiness, satisfaction and fulfilment. It is the time to enjoy the beauty of love, happiness, satisfaction and fulfillment. And thank the Nature and appreciate it for the blessings on you.

If anything wrong is happening with you and life is not moving in the direction you want, do not complain to Nature. You are spoiling the energy and sending negative thoughts to Nature and the same is being bounced back on to you. Whatever good you want, you must embrace it and what you do not want, do not complain against it; then you will be receiving more and more of what you want.

No matter what happens, never stop believing that you will somehow make it. Have an unrelenting belief that things will work out, that the long road has a purpose, that the things that you desire may not happen today, but they will happen one day; continue to persist and persevere.

Whatever you find in the world and whatever comes in your life, keep on praising them and blessing them. Whenever you praise or offer blessings; the vibrations of love flows in your body and mind. People who praise and bless all things which they receive such as health, happiness and accomplishment have full knowledge about blessings and praises. They recognize the power of the Nature. From now on awaken this energy in yourself and keep on blessing each and everyone who comes in to your life. Keep on igniting the lamp of love and the light of this lamp will enlighten you with hundred times more power. It will come back to you in multiple times.

By praising and blessing all the things your dissatisfaction and negativities vanish away. Once these evil thoughts vanish away, naturally positive thoughts return back with intensity. So you should keep praising your enemies, blessing them, and never think bad of them. You will feel and realize that the misunderstandings, differences and enmity have vanished away.

As you keep on blessing and see good things for others you will feel the lightness. **Very little is needed to make a happy life; it is all within you, in your way of thinking.**

******

Once you connect with some kind of higher purpose in your life, there will be a corresponding release of passion and energy.

The secret of generating extraordinary levels of passion in your life is to discover your larger purpose.

Once you find your calling, you get excited and begin to stand for something higher than yourself.

******

❐

Chapter-13
Magnetic Energy

To be born in the universe in this era is the best time, because this era has revealed the ancient secret for the first time and our heart has attained the wisdom to identify that every object, every being is energy. Entire universe, the whole galaxy, the earth including the parts within our body like kidney, liver, etc. are all made of cells. These cells are made of atoms which in turn are composed of electron, proton & neutron; which are nothing but energy. The conclusion is that whole universe is a synthesis of energy, power in all aspects is intermingled with each other and ultimately merges into Nature. Similarly energy is same for all existing things in Nature.

When you need anything then the vibration of the energy in you and the energy in the desired item intermingles or synchronizes, then those things come in front of you or is presented to you by Nature. You are like a magnet which is full of energy, as a result you attract the energy from the surroundings nearby you, so make yourself a powerful magnet of energy.

For the simple reason you do not know what kind of thoughts are running in others' mind. A scientist had quoted, *"The brain of human being does not alone consist of wisdom, but it is a power of connection that can collect small atoms and make them into a big one."* Actually, this is the power of universe which is consisting of small atoms converging into a big energy. Similarly by joining or adding our small assumptions and thoughts we can create anything.

You have immense power in yourself. You have to awaken this energy, which has so much power that it can tolerate all kinds of ups and downs and adversities coming in the life.

We keep ourselves limited to our physical body. We tell our bodies, "It is I or Me", it's a wrong concept. Your existence does not end over here. You are an unlimited source of energy. Energy is such a thing which can never be created nor destroyed, it can only change its form.

What is God? God is also an energy. It is a general belief that God always existed and will always exist. Neither it can be created nor can be destroyed. Simple conclusion is that God is energy and you are also the part of this energy. So you are a part of God. Therefore, never underestimate yourself. Know your values; you're the child of God, the almighty. You are energy and you are the part of the bigger energy. You always existed and you will always exist. But have to keep on transforming yourself. It can never happen that you will cease to exist.

You always remain immortal and your energy also remains immortal. It is impossible that you do not exist and your existence has ended in Nature. Just think and concentrate on energy. How you use the power of energy, to become optimistic or ruin it in pessimism?

We act and react according to the environment in which we live. We are forming our physique and environment according to our own choices and desires. Similarly we are writing our own destiny. The simple conclusion is that there is no end to our imaginations and creations. The energy in human being is limitless and unique. When he accumulates the power then he does experiments with that accumulated energy.

We all are one; one and the same energy is flowing in all of us. We are part of a big energy, and the basic energy is one and the same. You may call it God, you may call it Nature, you may call it creator, you may address it with any name but we are all part of one and the same. The time we admit this fact we will become perfect and we will achieve the perfectness i.e. we will be one with God, we will be one with Nature, we will be one with Creation.

You have to understand, that we create adversity for ourselves by thinking bad about others. Every action has an equal and opposite reaction. That action may be through a tangible act or thought. That's what Karma is. Even when you 'think' of harming others, it comes back to you in return. So think wisely and graciously. You are free to think whatever you want.

It is up to you to decide whether to think of harming a person or to shower a blessing upon him/her. If you doubt a person then it will come back to you with multiple force. Even a small thought of hopelessness is based on fear. The fear is due to the thought of attachment; we feel that we are getting separated from others.

This fear of not getting what you want results in jealousy. When a thought of competition enters in the person's mind he becomes conservative and thinks that there is a scarcity of things in Nature. You may start thinking what if the other person gets all the things. We fight and compete with each other for whatever is left in Nature thinking that there is scarcity and what will be left for me. If you jump in this competition then you take it for granted that you will never win in this competition. Even if you may feel that you have won, it will be an illusion. As per the law of Nature, when you have sown a seed of competition in Nature then it is evident you are inviting others to compete with you, thereby inviting further active and passive fights.

So never let the thought of competition enter your brain. When we are one unit, then whom are we competing with? Set aside the thought of competition and devote yourself in the field of creation. Concentrate on your dreams and on your positive attitude and root out the thought of competition from your mind.

Nature fulfills all needs and it is a supplier of unlimited material & opportunities. All the existing objects in the universe is the creation of Nature. You can get any of these materials through the Principle of Attraction. There is abundance everywhere. Let it flow to others through you.

When we think about anything then we attract it towards ourselves, this principle is also known as the Principle of Fulfillment. Under this principle you can attract any desired item of your choice from Nature. In case, if you think that you are not meeting such people who could help you and give you something, this is due to your own negative thinking.

As a matter of fact this invisible Nature fulfills your desires. The main source of all creation is the area of your energy. You may call this energy 'God', 'OM', 'Infinite' 'LIMITLESS' or 'WISDOM'; whatever you like. Whenever you accomplish or get anything, you must remember and realize that you have achieved this only because you had attracted these things for yourselves by the sense of attraction; that you had nurtured the seed of that particular item in Nature.

Another simple way of attracting the finest things in life is to realize that, ***'When you wish good for others, good things come back to you.'*** This is the unfailing law of Nature.

The power of Nature will move the entire universe to bring to you the right persons, right opportunities & right environment. You are a particle of God, so God has made you perfect like HIM. You are omnipotent and omniscient. You are a reflection of God. You are Energy. You are Wisdom. You are Perfect. You are flawless. You are Unique. You are the Creator.

Are you happy with what you have made out of your life, good or bad ? If not satisfied, this is the right time, change it immediately! You have the energy to turn your life in such a way that it will give you complete happiness. Few people think that they are the victims of the consequences of the environment. They were born in the family where parents used to quarrel with each other and curse themselves and remain in the state of adversity. It is the opinion of doctors that 85% of people have this kind of family environment. So majority of them cannot be different from others. Change your attitude and make your life positive. You do not need to continue the 'tough environment' you were born in. You can create a peaceful and loving environment for your children to grow up in. Work on betterment, not just in action but also in thoughts. What was happened in the past must not define your present or future; your trauma should not define you.

Always remember that when you are feeling good, you are powerfully attracting good things, more money & more abundance towards yourself.

❐

Chapter-14
Live in the Present

Life unfolds in the present moment. But so often, we let the present slip away, allowing time to rush past unobserved and un-seized and waste the precious seconds of our lives as we worry about future. "We are living in a world that contributes in a major way to mental fragmentation, disintegration, distraction, de-coherence." We are always doing something, and do not allow ourselves to practice stillness, calm and self love.

First of all we should love ourselves. When we do not love ourselves, it means we are getting ourselves separated from valuable things that we love. Whatever we want in our life is achieved only through love. Things such as youth, money, desirable partner, good jobs, healthy physique and beautiful body can be achieved if we spread love in nature. It has been noticed that it is very difficult for the people to love themselves. If you do not love yourself then you might have deficiencies within yourselves. Therefore, you can't make yourself prepared for the future.

When we are at work, we fantasize about being on vacation; on a vacation, we worry about the work piling up on our desks. We dwell on intrusive memories of the past or worry about what may or may not happen in future. We do not appreciate the present because our "monkey mind" wanders from thought to thought, like monkey swings from tree to tree.

Look into yourself. Realize yourself. Feel yourself, fully filled with eternal love for the present. Realize that your present is perfect, when you start thinking like this, you will automatically start loving yourself. As soon as you find any evil thought arising in yourself, shun it out and concentrate on your perfectness. Slowly and steadily all your evil thoughts will vanish away and the sense of peace will cover it up.

Most of us don't understand our own thoughts. Rather our thoughts control us. "Ordinary thoughts cross our mind are like a deafening water fall." In order to feel more control of our mind and lives, to find a senses of balance we need to pause, to become still - to stop doing and focus on just being in the present moment.

We need to live more in the moment, in a state of active, open intentional attention on the present. When you understand present, you realize that you are not what your thoughts are; you become an observer of your thoughts from moment to moment without judging them. People who live in the present are happier, more exuberant, more empathetic and more secure.

Living in the moment requires profound paradox; you can plan the future but not live in it.

There is no black board in the sky on which God has mentioned your target. So for what purpose you have come into this world?

It is because of what you desire? Your target is what you give to yourself. You make your life yourself. You fill the blackboard of your life at your own willingness. If you are filling this blackboard with rotten and evil thoughts, wipe it out immediately remove all the old thoughts and start a new life. Take a new slate or a new black board and start filling it from the beginning and from right now. Try to find out happiness, joy, rejuvenation, and enjoy the world. We have come in this universe to fill eternal love and happiness. From now onwards do only those acts which give you happiness and joy. Do not do any act which does not render you happiness.

"The secret of health for both mind and body is not to mourn for the past, or to worry about the future, but to live in the present moment wisely and earnestly", as was said by the Buddha. If you are not living in present, you are living in an illusion. This seems to be a pretty good reason to live in the present.

How often do we worry about things that are yet to come, how often do we beat ourselves up for the mistakes that we have made, no matter how much time has passed? We must realize the fact that living in present have good effect not only on our physical health but also on our emotional well being.

It's a fact that the amount of mental stress you carry can have detrimental impact on you health and overall well being. If you are living in present you are living in acceptance of events & when you are living in acceptance, you realize that everything is complete.

You can forgive yourself for the mistakes you have made in past and you can have peace within you heart to pursue further.

The worst part about living in the past or the future is that you are 'giving up' your personal power to live the life you want. If you are not living now, you are giving up your life. You are surrendering your power to create. If there are changes you would like to make in life, it is best to do it now. If you are living in the past, you cannot do anything about it, it's gone. If you are worrying about the future, you are living somewhere that does not exist. That hasn't happened yet. If you want to change your life, the only place you can do it is in the present.

But first you need to accept life as it is, when it comes down to it your mind is the only thing keeping you away from living in the present.

As discussed earlier, Nature identifies us with our thoughts, actually the dialogue inside our mind. We are the force that moves the universe. Knowing this, can help us overcome our fear and attain success.

There is a truth deep down inside you that has been waiting for you to discover, and that truth is this; you deserve all good things life has to offer.

To be able to receive it, clear you mind and soul of all negative thoughts.

******

Be Motivated!!

Motivation is knowing you are learning, growing and succeeding toward your desired outcome while sustaining positive.

******

❒

Chapter-15

From Past to Future

There was a well-to-do gentleman in our street; who was often found quoting, 'my parents were drunkard. They often called me filthy abuses. When I was six year old my parents got divorced... etc.' Many us might have passed through such troublesome situation. It means that one or the other person might have passed through such bad experiences. Now what would you like to choose? Old rotten memories or you would like to move ahead & not let the trauma dictate your life.

When people shun out bad memories, their life's purpose alter to create better opportunities.

The person who keeps concentrating and thinking about old bad times will be inviting those old sorrowful incidents again and again, this negative pattern of thinking will get him in depression, due to which he will not be able to create any good Karma, which will make him run around the repetitive cycles of criticism & unfulfilled ness.

Forget the past incidents that has happened with you, for your own sake. You can empower yourself with your own positive thoughts. Knowingly or unknowingly try to concentrate on the things which you want. Only these things or thoughts will let you feel the vibrations of love. You just have to start feeling these vibrations; Nature will do wonders for you.

You are writing your own destiny. You are writing your own story. The pen is in your hand and it is up to you that you write an interesting book out of it. The special thing about the law of Nature is that there is no delay in it. You can start whenever you like. You just have to sow the seeds of love, peace, satisfaction and unity in yourself and Nature will start moving along with you.

Nature's intelligence functions effortlessly and spontaneously, it is an intuitive, holistic and nourishing approach. When you are established in the knowledge of your own true self, you will rcalizc that in the Law of Nature there is no delay.

You can have any faith in mind, you will get it, as Nature is limitless. Always keep on thinking that you are young and growing younger day by day and will achieve whatever you want. Make it a belief that you will be able to free yourself from the webs of conservativeness, which were existing for many centuries. Get out of the superstitions, get out of the social taboos and hypocrisy, only then you will be able to prove that the energy within you is much more powerful than external worldly energies.

You may think I can't do it, I do not have enough money to accomplish all that. I am not enough competent, then remember that you are creating a vicious circle of scarcity around yourself.

When you say: I AM after these words whatever you had you are inviting that particular creation and that too with a big force. You are inviting a truth and a reality, when you claim with a command "I am tired", "I am late", "I am old", "I am bankrupt", then the Genie says, 'My Lord I am at your command, I will fulfill your desire.'

Knowing very well that these are not positive thoughts and we are wrongly using the word I AM. Should we not use these words for our benefit and positive thinking? Change it from today and starts saying, "I AM achieving the best things and thoughts from Nature, "I AM the happiest, I AM enjoying abundance, I AM fully accomplished, I AM fully healthy, I AM in state of love, I AM always in time, I AM energetic and immortal and always young. And I AM daily oozed with unlimited energy.

Be always energetic with new hopes, say to yourself - I AM complete, I AM robust, I AM powerful, I AM full of love, I AM full of happiness and I AM full of eternal peace. This law of nature can do anything for you. Have a faith upon your energy and rely on it that you have achieved whatever you had desired.

When Thomas Edison imagined of making a bulb, many people laughed at him and declared him mad. But Edison was intelligent. He had full faith in the law of nature. Today he has maximum inventions credited to his name. Edison said, "if you think you can do it, then you can definitely do it. And if you think you cannot, then definitely you will fail to do it. In both the conditions you are right. You achieved what you thought."

Do you think you cannot do, after knowing this secret? Now of course you can do, whatever you may want. Until now you may have not realized your values & internal energy; as people underestimated your ability. But now that you have realized your power and ability, you can achieve anything. Such as any invention, any inspiration, any answer, anything; whatever you desire you will achieve. You are unique and your wisdom is unparallel, you show yourself a mirror and try to recognize your true inner identity and the energy within yourself.

Is there any limit to it- no not at all. We have unlimited personalities. We have no bindings. Our capability, our art, our gifts and our power whatever is within us is unlimited and beyond bindings.

All the possibilities lie in the fact that you have realized the energy and you always keep it awaken in your mind and heart. If you open the doors of your brain, it will start flowing like a river. Within seconds it may drag you towards the uncomfortable incidents or take you to the future and spoil your tomorrow with bad experiences.

When you know that you are in the present and you have control over your thoughts, then take it for granted that you have accumulated unlimited energy in yourself. Ask yourself, 'What AM I thinking at present?' 'How AM I feeling now?' When you ask yourself such questions you are awakened because you have brought your brain to the present state. Whenever any thought arises, bring yourself to the present state. Repeat this practice minimum hundred times daily and remember that your entire energy lies in the fact that the energy in within you.

As soon as your brain wavers into multiple thoughts Nature gives you a hint or it pinches you to bring you back near to the Nature. Whenever you are not on the right path, Nature will give you indications such as you may hit somebody, you may hear a teasing sound, an alarm may ring, anything may slip out of your hand, these are the indications for the brain to bring you back to present state. Start noticing these indications. As soon as you realize that you are not in the present state you can bring yourself back to senses.

To realize the effect and the result of energy, you must experience the feeling of having that energy. Slowly and steadily you will find that you are getting the answers of your questions automatically. As you will start realizing the law of Nature, you may make it a habit to ask the answers of your questions. You will get all the answers of your questions, just open this book and you will find your answers on the page which opens.

The fact is that Nature is always replying your questions but you are not in a state of realizing it. Observe around yourself and remain awakened and you will be able to listen to the answers from Nature. You may get you answer through any source. It may be TV, Radio, a slogan on a truck, a book that you may lay your hands on, a conversation that is happening between two people, a newspaper heading, etc. The point is- you will be in a receiving state of getting your answer.

"The one who falls and gets up is so much stronger than the one who never fell."

******

We should understand ourselves to know what is meaningful to us, and what we want to devote our time to. This can be done by understanding our purpose, which takes dedication and patience. Reaching our purpose in life is a journey, not an event.

******

Chapter-16

Love, Liberty & Happiness

Love, liberty and happiness are there in life to be enjoyed. If you enjoy eating a *samosa* why do you leave it, eat and enjoy. Do not hesitate to do any act in which you find happiness. When you do any act with happiness, Nature gives you more and more opportunities and happiness keeps on flocking around you.

If you are depressed you are living in the past, if you are anxious you are living in the future. If you are at peace, you are living in the present. And Nature gives it to you in abundance. Happiness is based on what is happening around us and joy comes from things happening within us. Joy is a way of thinking. Joy is overall perception of life. It is internal happiness. There is no path to happiness; happiness is the path itself.

The actual secret of success lies in your internal happiness. You should be happy now, you should feel better now, this is all what you have to do in your life. If you enjoy any work, Nature gives you more and more of it. If you do not enjoy reading this book, leave it try another one. You are at complete liberty to do or not to do; you have to derive happiness from any act you are doing.

We miss things that we don't have. We miss things that we can't have. And through this pattern of missing, we miss looking after things that we have. Our experience of the world is heavily influenced by where we place our attention. Some people are afraid of allowing themselves to be happy because they think there is a negative event that will happen as a trade off. The truth is, bad things do not affect us as profoundly if we accept them with grace. That's true of good things too.

Your future is bright; there are unlimited possibilities, unlimited energy. We use only 5% of our brain and attain so much of knowledge; such as efficiency in medical sciences, engineering in astronomy, etc., you just imagine if we use 100% of our brain what could be the result! We would be able to do whatever we desire. We would achieve anything that we aspire.

This is a golden era of this universe. In this era, in every field and in every direction, we can see impossible becoming possible. Think in abundance, only then you will enjoy the uniqueness of unlimited utilities, this can be achieved in anyway: such as in the form of health, in science or any other chosen field of creation. Try to see yourself surrounded by good and positive things. All the religious books spread the same sermon, the more you enjoy the goodness and positiveness, the more the energy will increase.

You yourself are knowledge, you yourself are wisdom, you yourself are love and you yourself are a source of an eternal joy. You reach at this turning point of life for the simple reason that there is an eternal urge in yourself for this happiness and you have archived it. You are born to evolve in this world and to create happiness and prosperity.

Most of us wait our entire life for the appearance of a mythical kind of happiness, all the while missing the potential joy that was everywhere around us. Joy does not happen to us. It has to be created. We have to choose joy and keep choosing it every day; as joy attracts joy.

"I have to become more competent and more special than what I was yesterday." Whatever you had been doing up till now was to reach at the point where you are today. From now onwards you have to think what to do now, and imagine it. "How can I utilize each minute and second of the life. I have to prove my identity as nobody else can do any act other than me."

There is no miracle more impressive than a human being who is willing to admit that he is wrong and ready to learn something that will change his perspective, feelings, and behaviour.

You are genius. There is an uniqueness in you and you are born with a special ambition. Whatever may be your age, the moment you start thinking positively and in a right direction, an eternal energy will start flowing out to serve the purpose. Nature will start shaping your life with its own hands. It will feed you, it will dress you up, it will protect you and save your life.

Earth is revolving for you, rivers are flowing for you, birds are chirping for you, the sun rises for you, stars twinkle for you and anything beautiful in the world is acting for you. You are the Master of Nature and you are the successor of this Nature. There is always....... always a scope for betterment. You can not only change your life but of others too. Keep your heart clear & your soul free from all the blemishes.

Do not worry at all about negative thoughts, and do not try to control them. All you have to do is begin to think positive. Plant as many positive thoughts as you can every day. As you begin to think positive you will attract the goodness of life.

In order to perform a positive action we must develop a positive vision. Develop the inner vision and the habit of listening to the inner voice; and you are assured of peace, infinite joy and abundance of happiness. Life is not about creating yourself, life is about creating yourself. The present moment is filled with joy and happiness. If you are attentive, you will see it.

If you could wrap every thought in love, if you could love everything and everyone, your life would be transformed. Be in love with your life every minute of it.

Happiness isn't about getting what you want all the time. It's about loving what you have and being grateful for it. Love yourself first and everything will fall in place.

Joy is what happens to us when we allow ourselves to recognize how good things are. Remind yourself every day; "I am in-charge of my happiness. I will not let anything outside of myself to control me. I am creating a life that feels good on the inside and it will turn into experiences that are good on the outside."

You are an amalgamation of Love, Liberty & Happiness.

Love says: How great is our God;

Liberty says: It is well within my soul;

Happiness says: What a wonderful life I have!

******

Keeping balance in all situations is of utmost importance as it takes you to completeness. It is this balance that will make our journey through life smooth, effective & blissful. Happiness does not come automatically. We have to choose to live happily, we have to choose to live with integrity and we have to choose to conquering the daily battle and align ourselves with the purpose in Life.

******

❒

Chapter-17

Key to Happiness

I have heard people say, "I am rich, healthy and I am successful. But most of the time I feel I am not happy and I am still not satisfied?"

I have many clients, who have achieved success after success and are also happy and contended with their lives. When I asked the secret to a friend he said, "Every major breakthrough I have had in achieving my goals has come after a period where I ran out of motivation. I was in bleak situations and could not see any road ahead, I took a break for a few days and sometimes even a couple of weeks, and I came back to my goals with new vigor and energy." He took rest and he bounced back towards his goals. It is called resilience. It is one of the most important qualities of successful people, because it allows them to always go back towards their goals working with more aggression.

The other common trait of successful people is that when their goals are achieved they celebrate their success with their family and friends; rather they enjoy sharing the benefits and fruits with everyone around.

The key is to take the rest you need, and go right back to working towards your goals. Often, you'll find that the lack of motivation came from a lack of energy. Sometimes we work so hard towards our goals that we run out of gas and burn out. You will feel stuck or lost. And this situation is what we, as humans, see or visualize as un-happiness. In this situation there comes an imbalance of hormones in human body.

As per the latest medical research, for humans to be happy or feel happiness; a balance of four hormones (chemicals) in the body is required; namely Dopamine, Endorphins, Serotonin and Oxytocin. These hormones are released during various acts done by us. Let us discuss them one by one.

Endorphins: On your journey to become fit and healthy, your body releases endorphins to cope with the pain of physical exercise. When you probably began to enjoy exercise, as you got into it, and the endorphins makes you feel happy temporarily though.

Dopamine: When you work to become rich, you probably complete many tasks and goals. You may buy all the things you ever wanted or dreamed. Nice cars, beautiful clothes, and a perfect home. When you achieved your goals and bought these things your brain releases dopamine, which once again contributes to your happiness temporarily again.

But, what about the other two hormones? When and how are they released? It seems that human happiness is incomplete without all four chemicals constantly being released in the brain. To be completely happy, you need to work on releasing serotonin and oxytocin too. **Now the question is how do we do that?**

Serotonin is released when we act in a way that benefits others. When we give for a cause beyond ourselves and our own benefit. When we connect with people on a deeper human level selflessly; without expecting in return. While writing this book, serotonin is being released in my brain right now, because I am using my precious time to give back to others. Hopefully I am providing useful information through my book, that can help other people, like yourself.

We have often seen many billionaires turning to charity when they have already bought everything they wanted to, and experienced everything in life they wanted. They have had enough Dopamine from material pleasures and Endorphins from continuous success, now they need the serotonin.

On the other hand Oxytocin, is released when we become close to another human being. When we hug a friend, or shake someone's hand, oxytocin is released in varying amounts. Oxytocin is easy to release. It's all about becoming more social!

In nutshell, if you are rich and successful and still feel that happiness is not around you, I think it all comes down to the likelihood that you are missing two things: contribution and social connection.

Share your wealth with your friends and family to create amazing experiences. Laugh, love, cooperate, and play with others. Contribute to lives of people who are in need. Spare quality time for your family and friends. This will make you feel happy.

Happiness dosen't always come from taking but comes from giving; for sure.

Happiness is your nature. It is not wrong to desire it, what's wrong is seeking it outside when it is inside. It depends less on materialistic achievements and more on our attitude & thinking process.

******

When things are beyond your control and there is nothing you can do, why worry? "Worry never robs tomorrow of its sorrow, it only saps today of its Joy."

******

❒

Chapter-18

Rules of Success

Some people dream of success, while other people get up every morning and make it happen. Put your heart, mind and soul into even your smallest acts. Striving for success without hard work is like trying to harvest where you haven't planted. Stay positive, work hard & make it happen.

Humans are inclined to do things that give that satisfaction. We want to satisfy all our instincts. Be it related to food, mind or soul. But the attachment to this satisfaction has to switch away in time, if we are to evolve. Cutting what is not required will itself clear the clutter from your life & help in value addition. Once the land is fertile it is ready for the right seeds to be sown and cared after.

Complete the work in hand.

There is a shortage of time and work is in abundance but it is to be completed in a stipulated time. To make the work easy, first complete the work that you have been neglecting. You will get immense satisfaction after completion of work. And with great enthusiasm you will undertake the next job. In this manner you will keep on completing one work after another.

This division of work helps to expedite the work with ease and will give smoothness in success. It takes time to complete important and relevant task in life. This law also applies on our aims and goals which we want to achieve. Always classify your aims and targets, such as short term targets and long term targets. For short terms aims you may fix a period of six months and for long time targets you may set a period of five years. Be careful that both the targets cannot be achieved in a short time. It takes time to accomplish targets and they will be completed along with the time. These targets cannot be achieved by sitting idle. To achieve an aim there should be a determination and concentration .

Significator to Inspire You

To progress continuously in life both success and failure are the sources of inspiration. The biggest inspiration is achieved through defeat. Having being unsuccessful once, we are left with only one choice i.e. to reach at the peak. Do not put up the task for "Tomorrow". Complete it "Today" itself. To postpone the work for next day is the biggest obstruction in your success. We should not think what we are today. Rather we should think what we have to become tomorrow and how to become. Our aim should be clear and evident and there should be no dilemma regarding our achievement.

Self Confidence from Knowledge

Knowledge is power. It helps you to gain more confidence if we have knowledge of a particular task. Self confidence leads to success. Without knowledge we have a sense of fear within ourselves whether we will accomplish the job or not. Self confidence can help our thoughts of expression in an attractive manner. You should project only those views about which you are confident and bring out positive aspects of those views. You must not be over confident as it creates a sense of egoism. Due to a sense of pride, we try to hide the truth of our life and to fulfill the egoism we take shelter of false imagination and fake methods.

Change Your Vision

If you have a positive attitude in mind you will definitely achieve success and reach your goal. When you start any work with a negative vision then you fail to dedicate yourself with full heart. As a result you may face many obstructions and fail to achieve the target. You should always keep a positive vision and determination. Even at the time of difficulties you should have a determination that time will be favourable and you will succeed.

Effective Conversation

The exchange of information and knowledge is known as conversation. It means that we should express ourselves in an effective manner and use proper words. We communicate with each other with the medium of words and these words form a forceful expression.

Expressions should be such that they should touch the heart of others but not hurt them. Satirical expression may hurt others, so you should be very selective in using words. The expression of words give life to the thoughts of our inner self. Before answering to anybody you must pay complete heed to your speech. It saves both time and words.

In this era we are living in the basis of the knowledge of international, financial system. So it becomes more essential that we succeed in our aims. To achieve success we must accomplish our work within the stipulated time. Before speaking we must select appropriate words. Then with full knowledge, confidence and with the positive attitude we should put forward our thoughts, the arrow of our thoughts will strike at the target.

"There are no secrets to success. It is the result of preparation, hard work and learning from failure; beside firm belief in the power of Nature."

-Colin Powell
Former General & National Security Adviser
United State of America

You can have unbelievable intelligence, you can have connections, you can have opportunities failing out of sky. But in the end, the right mind set is the true, enduring characteristics that will take you to the goal.

Success begins in the mind and is fulfilled in the hands of consistent hard work. As long as you are willing to work hard on you mind, you can attain anything in this life; may be with some struggles. But those struggles will look like petty obstacles from a higher vantage point.

Yes, that's what we have been talking about. A higher vantage point. A higher standard of living. A higher standard of thinking. A higher state of being. A high life, all together. Not just for you, but for every one around you.

As you heal yourself, so do you heal the entire universe When one person achieves a higher state of consciousness, he/she is the consciousness of the world.

We are sure our enlightened readers will listen to their heart and appreciate that dreams are sent to be followed & life is meant to be enjoyed. This small treatise will make them believe in themselves, become an instrument of God, to help the soul of the world and understand why they have been sent on this beautiful planet.

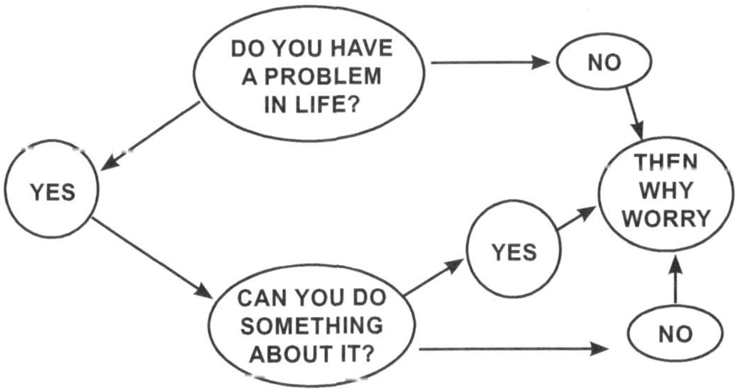

❑❑❑

Best Selling Books
By Pt. Gopal Sharma, B.E.

108 Golden Tips (for Love, Health, Wealth and Success)

Are you facing troubles related to friendship, love and romance, family, money, children, education or business? Are you suffering from health or legal problems? You can now say good-bye to them.

This book contains 108 miraculous tips to achieve better relationships with society, colleagues and family members. The book features trusted and tested ancient remedies that enhance your physical and mental capabilities and open the golden door to ensure health, wealth and happiness around you. This edition is available in both English and Hindi languages.

Golden Sutra of Success

Inspiring the readers, this book specifically explains the qualities that make success easy by leaving behind despair and desperation.

This miraculous research work, will surely encourage you to succeed and teach new skills and ensure a happy and prosperous life; which encourages positive thinking and capacity to march ahead in life.

Ways to Attract Wealth

To live a successful life, every person needs a healthy body, a simple and stress-free business/job, besides needed means of comfort and convenience in the house.

This happy and successful life is not possible without the blessings of Goddess Mahalaxmi.

What simple means should be adopted to attract positive energies and wealth to every home? This is what this unique book on Vedic Vastu Shastra by the renewed Vaastu engineer Pt. Gopal Sharma; tells us in simple and lucid words.